Unwin Education Books: 23

EDUCATION AND THE COMMUNITY

Unwin Education Books

Series Editor: Ivor Morrish, BD, BA, Dip.Ed. (London), BA (Bristol)

Other books by Eric Midwinter

Unwin Education Books: 23

Series Editor: Ivor Morrish

Education and the Community

ERIC MIDWINTER

London

GEORGE ALLEN & UNWIN LTD

RUSKIN HOUSE   MUSEUM STREET

First published in 1975

ISBN 0 04 370065 9 hardback
     0 04 370066 7 paperback

Composition by Linocomp Ltd, Marcham, Oxon

Printed in Great Britain
by Redwood Burn Limited Trowbridge & Esher

To Catharine

Contents

Introduction

An ageing yarn tells of the seven-year-old youngster who, while doing his homework, confronted his father with the poser: 'Daddy, where did I come from?' Like parents before and since, he reviewed the dilemma. Should he reveal all or stick with the myths? He had read of sex education films in the junior school, almost as if the much-prized 'discovery' method, which had served many in its time, had grown redundant. Contrarily, he had read of commentators who managed to rank sex education and Danish Blue on the same pornographic menu. So he stayed with the legends. 'Son,' he said, 'the stork brought you in a white sheet.' The boy pursued his tack. 'Where did you come from, daddy?' he enquired. 'The doctor brought me in a Gladstone bag', the father explained. At that moment the child's grandmother entered, and he put the question to her. Daddy tipped her a wink, and, with the shrewd mental agility of grannies throughout history, she caught on immediately. 'I was found', she announced solemnly, 'under a gooseberry bush at the bottom of the garden.' The boy finished his homework and retired to bed, and the father, alive to the needs of well-informed home-school relations, decided to read his son's little essay. It began: 'As far as can be safely ascertained by puristic, scientific investigation, there has been no sexual intercourse in our family for at least three generations.'

The father had mistaken a general social factor for a specific educational point. He had forgotten that children learn all the time and from all sources, and that what traditionally has been regarded as 'educational' (that is, the academic element of the school) is but a part of this. The social context in which schooling occurs is more important than the schooling apropos—and this is the savagery of the irony—the actual schooling itself. Because the totality of a child's experience, from birth and from every quarter, contributes to the manner and quality of his achievement in school, the school itself is often no more than an agent of affirmation.

For the majority of children one can make fairly accurate prognostications, simply from a knowledge of the accident of their birth.

One can, for too vast a majority, anticipate, not only how they will fare scholastically, but what sort of height, health, jobs, spouses and, sorrowfully, children they will enjoy or otherwise. It is this prophetic character about our social system which explains what has rightly been called 'the cycle of deprivation', and, by the same token, it explains 'the cycle of affluence'. It explains what, despite the many exceptions, must be seen as a hereditary characteristic persisting in our society.

The final phase of this coming realisation about the nature of the education process has occurred over the last twenty years. It had long been noted and accepted that what often had been the privilege of education had been bestowed by the already privileged on their off-spring. It was believed, naively in the event, that if the opportunity was accorded at all, then privilege would be, in the case of education, vanquished and the ramifications of that conquest would affect the rest of the social commonwealth. This was the ultimate educationist's arrogance: despite the fact that education would be unaffected by social factors, it would, nonetheless, affect those social factors itself.

There is no doubt that, in a technical and legal style, the promise of equal opportunity has been reasonably well kept, in so far as no child is barred, socially or economically, from a full negotiation of the educational process. But the consequence of this equalisation of technical and legal opportunity has been disappointing, and the overall irony of schooling has been revealed.

Social composition remains a firmer guide to educational form than type of education. One can estimate, from a knowledge of the social classification of a district, approximately the numbers of its children who will obtain the nap hand of five O-levels, stay on in the sixth form or move on to higher education. Knowing that an area has this or that type of secondary organisation is much less useful a piece of information. Study, for example, the following figures.

	Population in Social Classes I and II %	Population in Social Classes IV and V %	Age-Group in 6th Form %	Age-Group in Higher Education %
United Kingdom	20	30	19	7
Wallasey	20	28	19	7
Bristol	17	28	19	7
Solihull	36	14	27	19
Barnet	34	17	35	16
Newham	9	38	10	3
Barking	9	36	9	3

Wallasey and Bristol, which, in social class terms, form a sort of miniature United Kingdom, have very nearly the same rates of educational striking. The more upper-crust—Solihull and Barnet—and the more bottom-drawer—Newham and Barking—are appropriately educated for better or for worse.

All in all, the number of sixth-formers has doubled in the last twenty years, but the proportion of working-class sixth-formers remains obdurately the same. The proportion of working-class youth in higher education—and this includes the polytechnics—is only marginally more than it was in 1926, the year of the General Strike. Given a cross-the-board sample of one hundred children, the thirty middle-class pupils (Classes I, II and IIIa on the Registrar-General's scale) will produce twelve with five O-levels apiece, while the seventy working-class pupils (Classes IIIb, IV and V) will produce only eight. The business executive's or manager's son has a seven-to-one shot of higher education; the miner's or postman's son has a thirty-five-to-one shot.

In the railway journey of life the school is the waiting-room rather than the signal box. It is a kind of sociological Calvinism by which the child's destiny is frequently dictated, for good or ill, by his social constraints. Eton does not change ordinary schoolboys into foreign secretaries with the flourish of the legendary magician transforming frogs into princesses. Eton is a stretch of that particular avenue of life along which future foreign secretaries have been routed. The city secondary school is, by the same measure, no more responsible for the unemployment and poor housing and juvenile delinquency of its clients than the public school is responsible for the disasters of our cabinet ministers.

Put another way, schools cannot be held to be the scapegoat of social dislocation, nor can the lack of, or 'wrong', education be held culpable for social troubles. Such a hypothesis heavily overestimates the ability of the school to alter people or affairs. There are schools in deprived districts where, in spite of brilliant teaching, the children produce poor results. There are schools elsewhere in which the children perform brightly in spite of outmoded teaching.

It is possible to analyse the components of the social context which so compellingly influences a child's educational performance. One cannot, of course, deny some genetic element, although, if that be elevated to the heights of an absolute explanation, it posits a dark, malevolent cloud descending on Bootle, leaving the Midwich Cuckoo-land of nearby Southport untouched. It is to do with income, with culture, with life-style, with peer-groups, with aspirations, with facilities, with housing, with parental know-how and drive, and with a dozen other features. They add up to a devastating paradox about the nature of education, so much so that we must reverse the normally received equation. Once we thought of the school educating, and the rest intervening where possible. We must now accept that it is the rest—the community, more particularly the home—which educates, and it is the school which is forced to adapt and come to terms where it may.

The school, as is the nature of institutions, is reluctant to change. This is understandable, for this is defeatist talk: if attainment is pre-determined, what price the teacher? It is not quite as tidy as that, how-ever. The school is not in neutral gear. By remaining an agency in seclusion, proffering its wares in something of a social vacuum, in the belief that its academic product has an exclusive being of its own, it has helped maintain and perpetuate the existing system.

The school has, by and large, a single cutting-edge, despite the many —but usually superficial—differences up and down the country. It serves a multivariant society, and it offers that society very much the same product everywhere. This would not be too bad if the product were alien to all; if it were, so to speak, equally estranged from every-body. But it is not. It has a built-in tendency to find a communion of values, aims, culture and so forth with the Richmonds rather than the Warringtons of our world. We have uniformity, rather than equality, of opportunity, and that uniformity has a Barnet rather than a Barking-bias.

This is not said critically of teachers or administrators, who work unceasingly to bring succour to less privileged environs. It is because education, along with all the other forms of social outlay, forms an intricate mesh of social provision. We have too often analysed educa-tion in a crude cause-effect sequence. Either the school has changed or created society, or society has changed or created the school. These are simplistic views. It is much more a circular process in which the elements both underwrite and are underwritten in cyclic sequence. Thus one would scarcely expect schools to be more fluently aligned with the under- than the over-privileged, just as we would hardly predict that the health service or the legal system might be more valuable for the poor than the rich.

The chief lesson is the interdependability of all forms of social pro-vision. Just as health, good or bad, affluence or otherwise and so on affect education, so is any of those influences affected in turn by an amalgam including education. We more or less accept that health cannot be observed independently: nor should education logically be examined in an autonomous fashion. If a child is ill, we may look for causes in poor housing or malnutrition; only recently have we, and then usually only in the extreme cases of 'problem' families, admitted the crucial effect of such factors on schooling. Even when we have done this, our approach has been negative. We have assessed how the child has *not* been educated, how his schooling has been impeded by extraneous factors; less readily have we acknowledged the input of what we would regard as adverse conditions, that is the 'educational' messages of one sort or another transmitted to the child by those conditions.

It is important to see education in this total sense, as a dimension with which, knowing or unknowing, we are in constant communication. One does not, for instance, have a period of 'non-health'. One has, obviously, some form of health perpetually. The question is about its quality and its degree of badness or goodness. Similarly, education should be seen not as something one did, but as something one is, like health, 'in'!

The sticking-point is our long-held 'apprenticeship model' of education, whereby we have viewed it as the preparation of the young for society to the point where leaving school has adopted some of the aura of the initiation ceremonies of older societies. Education is over-geared, in our image, to children in school and students in colleges. But it is, in reality, total and constant, partly because we continue learning in some form or another, and partly because we all contribute, in more or less degree, to the learning of others, especially children. Each individual has a kind of current account with the educational bank, with deposits as well as withdrawals.

Once this is accepted, the interconnectedness of social provision follows. We remark the interconnection of social ills; rationally, an interconnected treatment might be a consequence.

Society has normally been heir to four categories of social ill. This macabre quartet comprises poverty, disease, crime and ignorance. These are the four horsemen of the social apocalypse. They represent the chief ways in which individuals or groups fall short of the norms current in their society. For whatever reason, the social casualty is, to resort to educational jargon, an 'under-achiever'. For whatever reason, he has less income or goods than is normatively needed in his society; his state of health hinders him, even prevents him from fulfilling the expected role of the citizen in his society; he will not or cannot meet the legal requirements deemed necessary by his society for the sustenance of its stability; his skills and knowledge are inadequate for him to cope normally in his society. Usually, of course, two, three or all brands of social difficulty are present in a cumulative form.

In practically all societies there is evidence of arrangements to deal with these problems. Sometimes the treatments—like the troubles—have been co-ordinated. Perhaps education has been linked less than the others, and that perhaps because of its early critical phase. In other words, whereas poverty, crime and disease are very evident in adulthood, the issue of ignorance has frequently, if misleadingly, been restricted to childhood. Nonetheless, social provision in many societies has encompassed all four areas.

Often the act of co-ordination has been deliberate, as when some bold policy or comprehensive formula has been implemented by the governing body. Possibly more frequent have been examples of an unconscious togetherness. This is because social ills and, by projection, social provisions are automatically characteristic of their socio-economic context. The evils themselves are perpetual—the poor are always with us—but their shape and fashion vary. The life-styles of the impoverished in the Scottish Highlands of the eighteenth century and in modern Calcutta are different. The colour of these life-styles is determined by their respective socio-economic formats. Consequently, what is attempted to assist them is dictated by those same constraints, not least because the question is posed within these constraints. One might go further and argue that, even when some apparently clear-cut governmental policy has emerged to meet a range of problems, this has also been created by the context it serves.

The inability of a piece of social provision, such as education, to escape the dictates of its social and economic bounds is an important consideration. It cannot be accomplished purely and in a vacuum. Any theoretical notion or practical proposal for education must meet the strict ordering of its social confines, otherwise it becomes, at best, shallow and false, and, at worst, disruptive and damaging.

Another reason, naturally enough, for the apparent coherence of social policy has been, in most societies, the control exercised by one group or class over another. The incidence of social ills, or at least their most troublesome ramifications, has generally fallen most heavily on the governed rather than the governors, on the unprivileged rather than the privileged. It was mentioned earlier that none need be surprised by this. Those in control do, to a large extent, outline normalcy in terms of social policy; almost by so doing they avoid overdue contravention; and they can ensure that social and economic regulos are suitable for their own well-being. Indeed, *not* to be suffering from social ills is not much less than saying you are well-placed in the social, political and economic hierarchy.

Peoples get, therefore, the social provision they deserve, and that includes education. Their type of society governs, that is, the type of social treatment meted out to them. We have probably, in education, been long in error about this, viewing the problem in isolation as a puristic and academic consideration. Of course there have been administrative and other practical devices envisaged, but have they always investigated, deliberately and consciously, their valid and proper relationship with their social and economic surrounds?

It could be argued that, by seeing the school and the education authority as academic things-in-themselves, teachers and educational administrators have been out-manoeuvred. A system has resulted, which, by a mixture of default and accident, does reflect some of the needs and some of the traits of our society. As was argued above, it could hardly do otherwise: the character of an institution must inextricably be flavoured by its host society. But if the education system could be consciously steered, with open eye, towards meaningful and aware integration with all social provision, indeed with all social and communal development, then hopes for a more productive pay-off might be raised.

If education recognised its place in the cycle—in part manipulated by and in part manipulating the rest of social provision—it would mean a move from the rather restricted bureaucracies of the day, busily guaranteeing the legal and technical requirements of school accommodation and attendance. This is not to say that the incumbents of the bureaucracies wish it this way. We are all, to some extent, imprisoned by the remorselessly cabining effect of attempting to operate a blinkered system. Rather might there be release for the inmates—both teaching and administering—of that system, if it could be aligned more fluently and purposefully with its natural social and economic environs.

The aim here is to examine further the nature of social provision, with the purpose of developing a frame of reference for the reform of our educational mechanics. Thereafter there will be detailed discussion of these reformed educative devices, and, in conclusion, an effort will be made to realign these in turn on the fuller spectrum of social provision and communal development.

Chapter 1

The Historical Development of Educational and Social Provision

The extreme pessimist might gloomily argue that the education system is totally determined by the character of society. The supreme optimist might gaily contend that the world is the educational administrator's oyster, and he can create the system he wishes. The middle and, hopefully, saner view is that the process is cyclic and occasionally developmental. One can, that is, innovate and change within the margin left by social and other determinants and in so doing, those very margins are altered. This could allow for a developmental factor in which the knowledge and experience garnered may have an accumulative effect on the system. Thus an understanding of how the situation (with which one has, as teacher or administrator, to grapple) came to pass is important in any appraisal of that situation. Neither the austerity of pristine theory nor the enthusiasm of 'good practice' are of value unless they can meet in harmony with the organic context of the issue faced.

Herein should lie the virtue of the much-maligned 'History of Education', characterised too often in the past by undue concern with legislation. The 'History of Education' course has frequently resembled the baseball batter, desperately racing against time around a diamond whose bases are set at 1836, 1870, 1902 and 1944. A more helpful approach for the educational historian would be to provide students, teachers, officers and committee members with the skills to adjudicate historically. For example, each teaching situation represents a fluid and organic amalgam of inheritances from days gone by. To make intelligible assessments about the current reading scheme, the crate of milk in the corner, the number of children in the class, and all the other humdrum points, requires a grasp of why it was implemented and why it has perished. Without such an evaluative tool, one might be misled into thinking in terms of sheer accidents or, much worse, into assuming everything was originally done for sound and persisting educational reasons.

This use of perspective to adjudge policies for educational change is all the more important when the overall structure of a local authority is under consideration. A community, such as the ambit of a local education authority, has many unique traits, but, in some of its basics, it may well be similar to most other communities distant from it in time and space. This is especially true if one accepts the hypothesis that the type and format of any education system is, at the very best, flavoured, along with other forms of social provision, by the society it serves. It is possible, and it is useful, to trace some of this cycle of interplay between society and its social provision, to observe the emergence of our own twist in the spiral, and to watch for general principles which might assist in forward planning.

If the life-span of the earth were represented as a calendar year, man would not appear until 31 December, and then hardly in time for tea. The Neolithic breakthrough would occur at about eleven-thirty, and Jesus would be born two minutes before midnight. Twenty seconds would separate the discovery of America by Columbus from the loss of the American colonies by the British.

The social and educational problems facing the world must first be seen in this context. Society is worldwide now, and the question of social provision facing it is akin to the classic survival drama beloved of film-makers and variously located in lifeboat, desert or beleaguered fort. Supplies of food and water being limited, do the strong push overboard the wounded, old and feeble in order to ensure that some at least reach safety, or is there a general but necessarily thin share-out in the hope that all might survive? It should be recalled that the creature judging this question spent over 90 per cent of his existence in prehistorical times, and, despite the obvious inadequacies of evidence, one should begin the history of social provision there. The social and economic history of man begins with his birth, for social and economic needs are immediate, and the social ills consequent upon insufficient resources must be almost as old.

The brutishness of man is as self-evident as it is discouraging. For all but less than a tenth—perhaps for all but 1 per cent—of his existence, man has been a carnivore and sometimes a headhunter. Scratch an American business tycoon or a Chinese cadre leader and you may find a cannibal. Some commentators have excused our ancestors their cannibalism on the grounds of religion, suggesting that eating one's dead enemy was a symbolic mark of triumph and of the acquisition of his talents. This theological apologia, reminiscent of the final stanzas of 'Ilkley Moor b'aht'at', seems, however, more revolting than plain straightforward hunger. And early man's hunger knew few bounds. It is confidently reported that man, nature's chosen scavenger, has partaken of hyena flesh, a delicacy with which no other bird nor beast, not even another hyena, has been able to cope.

For thousands of years, until the coming of agriculture, man existed by predatory methods, either collecting the vegetable bounty around him, or hunting down animals or fish. It has been calculated that such a precarious living could have accommodated only two people per square mile, and that, before agriculture, the population of the world hovered, in very approximate terms, around ten millions. Man, like his forbears, is a gregarious animal. Such higher forms of life involve a necessarily lengthy phase of immaturity (that is, more positively, 'schooling') in their young, in order that the physical and other developments may occur that are essential to so complex an existence. The young ape, for instance, spends three years with his mother, and is not able to reproduce until ten years of age.

Thus biological and economic circumstances coupled with socio-logical and psychological beliefs to form communal societies; indeed, some would regard the needs of a predatory economy as dictating the communal morality. Certainly private ownership was and is at a discount in primitive society, and, just as the hunting party functioned co-operatively, so were the proceeds of the chase divided on roughly egalitarian lines, with occasional tastier or larger morsels perhaps given to the older or stronger. Sometimes trinkets or weapons might be personally owned, but, in the main, the primitive society func-tioned collectively, both in production and consumption. Living ac-commodation was equally a communal venture, and some evidence points to primitive sex-life enjoying the same engaging air of the ensemble. These were small groups, endlessly roaming probably huge tracts of territory for fruit and game. The prehistoric has been called an affluent society, with its lucky members feasting off a high protein diet and with lots of time available for leisure pursuits. Its passing has been bemoaned by those who regard the routine drudgery of agricul-ture, to say nothing of the purported ennui of industry and urban life, as destructive of man's natural verve. The truth was undoubtedly less happy, with the fight for survival ever uppermost, and the pressure so harsh that immersion in the group was the only answer.

What, then, of social provision in this first 99 per cent of man's story? Was there a need for it, what form did it take, and who pro-vided it? The evidence is so frail that one can do little more than con-tinue to bandy speculation, in the pious hope that the guesses are reasonably bright. To begin with, how might prehistoric man have conceived of the major social ills of poverty, disease, crime and ignorance?

There are no absolutes with social ills. Poverty can be starvation or it can be not having a second car and an annual trip to the French Riviera. Ill-health can be dying of cancer or missing a visit to the theatre because of a slight headache. Even crime, most definitive of social ills, has its relativity. The Spartan boy who stole the fox and let it gnaw his breast rather than admit it—he was a folk-hero, and specialised theft was a Spartan virtue. Most people would judge differently the mother stealing crusts in a concentration camp and the Great Train Robber. Ignorance can be not being able to read the racing columns of the daily paper, only managing a third-class degree, or living in an Iron Age fort and not knowing how to start a fire.

Social ills are, like beauty, in the eye of the beholder. We make value-judgements based on a personal yardstick or on the yardstick of our own community. The Glaswegian slum-dweller lives in poverty compared with the motor car manufacturing executive in Solihull. But, if the beggar in Bombay is introduced into the assessment, then the slum-dweller is judged to wallow in luxury. Social ills are also in the eye of the victim as well as in that of the beholder. A poorly-paid worker feels poverty-stricken and is perhaps embittered by it. His assessment is immediate and localised. He is comparing with his more highly-paid boss; he possibly fails even to contrast his lot with that of his father in the 1930s. The same duality exists with health. The hypochondriac feels terribly poorly, but everyone else thinks him exceedingly fit.

Social ills, therefore, reflect distinctions drawn according to personal judgement in a certain set of circumstances. These distinctions are in constant flux, from community to community, from time to time, from person to person, and within the same person at different times about different cases. This may well be the heavy labouring of a trite point, but there is sufficient glib reference to poverty or crime to make its rehearsal useful. The idea of distinction is of such prior meaning. At its extreme, the one-man band, the recluse effectively cut off from all human contact, cannot conceive of social ill. He cannot suffer poverty nor ill-health, and he cannot commit crime nor be ignorant. There may be ethical and theological objections to this conclusion, but, in social terms, it can hardly be denied.

In prehistoric times man appears to have been largely involved in a singularity of existence. A frequently egalitarian economy, a severe social nexus, a frightening psychological pressure, a firm moral code —these were some of its ingredients. The incidence of social ills would be according to the totality of that submergence of individualism characteristic of many pre-civilised groups. Where it was complete, social problems would be negligible. The unity of such a primitive society could be compared to the recluse or hermit. Distinctions would not be possible faced with that awesome oneness. Poorer, sicker, naughtier, duller, become meaningless, for there must be a two-some before comparatives are feasible. In its ultimate, the primitive tribe could not, presumably, think or feel in terms of social deprivation.

Indeed, in most studies of primitive man, it must be confessed that few signs of an appreciation of poverty, disease, crime and ignorance are discernible. There are some pointers. Disease was an inevitable experience for primitive man, but it resolved itself, abruptly and briskly, into the quick and the dead—a heavy infant mortality rate apart, possibly only a half lived beyond their mid-twenties. Crime was possibly the most definite social problem of the four but, even with crime, offences tended to be political-cum-religious, private affronts against the public weal. Strangely, poverty, which has caused such anguish throughout history, was hardly an issue while, as for ignorance, there was normally a stock of practical know-how and a corpus of religious and social information common to all. If social evils were to be the consequence of distinction and comparison, then civilisation, even in its crudest early form, was to produce such gradations. Only with stratification could the concepts of poorer, sicker, less clever and more criminal properly develop.

Although 'civilised' carries overtones of culture and behaviour, it is obvious that economic change was a major, if not the primary, factor involved. This economic revolution occurred when man moved from the food-gathering or Mesolithic to the food-producing or Neolithic stage. Pre-civilised man had developed certain techniques, like tool-making and the use of fire, but they had merely acted as useful aids to his predatory nature. Indeed, by increasing his efficiency as hunter with such skills, he may well have endangered his survival by over-indulging the animal and vegetable bounty at his disposal. Such a consideration may well have played its part in the initiation of the Agricultural Revolution. By controlling the growth of plants and by the domestication of animals for draught power as well as food, man was able to extend his food supply and, just as rewarding, increase its dependability.

So far the earliest discovery of agricultural remains has been those at Jericho, where Neolithic evidence has been dated at about 7,000 BC. Other evidence confirms that the Near East was the seat of this great economic change, and that it dates about nine thousand years ago. What is sure is that, over the next thousands of years, agriculture spread throughout the world. By 2000 BC agrarian economics had been inaugurated in most of Europe, and soon, by historical standards, the farmers were many and the hunters were few. Since that time agriculture has improved its efficiency endlessly.

The social concomitants of this immense change were varied. Probably the most far-reaching was the demographic explosion which agriculture sustained. Most agrarian societies seem to have been capable of maintaining high birth-rates of 3 to 5 per cent, and, despite comparably high death-rates, the life expectancy of their members was more encouraging than that of their predatory counterparts. By 1750, on the eve of the so-called Industrial Revolution, world population had sprung from a very approximate 10 million in 10,000 BC to a very approximate 700 million. When it is recalled that this agricultural phase lasted no more than 1 to 2 per cent of man's existence, then the full magnitude of this demographic phenomenon may be realised.

A further social factor was settlement. The predatory economy inferred a considerable amount of nomadism and shifting habitation. The control of the environment in agricultural terms necessitated a much more stationary existence. It betokened the advent of village life and eventually of urban life. At first settlements were not much larger than the camps of the earlier predators. The growth of population manifested itself not so much in the size as in the number of units. Instead of a few, widely-scattered groups of hunters, there developed many more settled groups of farmers. The Jericho settlement was no more than about ten acres, and purely agricultural groups seldom numbered more than a few hundred.

The combine of increased population and the settled life led to a mild paradox, for, although nomadism decreased, migration was accelerated. Agriculture was spread not only by imitation but by migrant bands practising the new skills in new lands. As the techniques improved, so was the utilised land extended, while increasing population made such an extension necessary. Inevitably, too, the premium on wandering rose and fell according to whether the agriculture was pastoral or arable, and the more settled character of grain cultivation was to be in incessant contest with the more unsettled nature of cattle breeding.

Another social effect of far-reaching importance was the conception of ownership. The connection of man and land or livestock may well have been originally on a communal basis, but differentiation of ownership soon evolved. In practice a clan or household would be accepted as the cultivators of a particular area, and finally this would, at least to their satisfaction, bestow a claim on it. Ownership of agrarian implements must also have developed, and a much more sophisticated idea of property was thereby created.

These social elaborations, together with settlement and larger communities, eventually required management on quite a complicated scale. To revert to the example of Jericho, the organisation of three thousand souls into a community reliant on irrigated fields presumably required a political regulo. Building and engineering are implicit in Jericho's scheme of things, and this necessitated successful management. Funereal and military erections throughout the world testify to well-organised communities in Neolithic times. A function of leadership was presumably the enforcement of property rights and the regulation of local customs relating to ownership. Stability in the agricultural society must depend on security of tenure in order to assure the farmer that it is worthwhile preparing the soil for future returns. As well as the normal duties of defence and internal order, leadership often must have involved not only the organising of an economic pattern but its subsequent maintenance.

From the facet of political organisation to the facet of the written record was a simple step. Literacy—often used as a criterion of civilisation—was a product of Neolithic society. The intricacies of life were clarified by record. Laws, farming returns, government business, military schedules and a dozen other items could be committed to some form of writing. Further specialisations would abound in the shape of scribes and notaries. And yet 'writing was a temple invention'. The intellectual life of primitive man had been in the main magico-religious, and this trend was not changed, only complicated, by the new agricultural communities.

This religiosity had invariably a strong link with governance. The chief or king might be regarded as god or, less ambitiously, as god's representative. The functions of chieftain and priest might well have been shared, and there must normally have been a strict correlation between religion and law, with the divine beatifying the civil power. The intellectual impetus of religion gave it a flying cultural start, and writing, for the literary glorification of the supernatural and the codification of supernatural tenets, was the instrument of the priesthood. The literacy essential to the elaborate agrarian structure was in priestly hands, and these hands thus supervised the usage of writing, in government and business, and its transmission to others; that is, they affirmed their watch on education. Whether priests invented writing because they were also bureaucrats or became bureaucrats because they had invented writing is a moot point. What is sure is that the politico-religious direction of agricultural communities was constant and firm and that literacy affirmed this connection. The concept of the Pharaoh was to illustrate the high watermark of this proclivity, and, of course, the theocratic element in early government also occurs in cultural aspects other than writing. Advanced art and political and theological forms might well have predated agriculture, but it is agriculture which permitted of their sustenance and progress. Economic survival is the self-evident prerequisite of politics and culture—the dead do not write and paint. Agriculture relieved some men from the constant battle with mere survival. It allowed populations large enough to encourage specialisation of many kinds and increased prosperity allowed some men the freedom to develop technical, cultural and governmental skills.

Civilisation, then, as understood here, describes a condition of life in which, on balance, man produces rather than gathers food, has begun manufacturing and using a variety of tools, is more rather than less settled into organised political community, is reproducing himself with more or less greater competence, has some form of written recording, has developed some type of supernatural commitment and has created a reasonably sophisticated culture.

Of the early agricultural communities it is the Hebrews who, through the medium of the Old Testament, are most familiar to the Western reader. Although they are normally remembered by such readers on a plane of reality other than the historical and although they were a people who have never been regarded as among the more exotic or substantial of ancient civilisations, their well-known story may aptly serve to illustrate the theme of this chapter.

The Psalms, attributed to the shepherd David, indicate the agrarian, chiefly pastoral, character of Hebrew life. They were, as the Mosaic narrative implies, concerned with settlement in an area conducive to the prosperity of their flocks. The constant arising of leaders at critical times, such as Moses, Gideon or Abraham, and their arrangement into tribes testify to the political organisation of the Hebrews, and their deliverance and migration from Egypt and eventual construction of towns testify to its success. The Old Testament itself is witness to their adoption of the literate record, and its variety—legal, historical, literary, prophetic—is very noticeable. Their art-forms, especially in the field of literature, were well advanced, and they had developed a highly complex and severe legal system, as the Pentateuch indicates. They enunciated a religious interpretation—that of monotheism—which is usually regarded as their greatest contribution to civilisation. They attempted an explanation of the creation of the universe and of the meaning of man's place in it. They attempted to align social and theological morality as in the Ten Commandments. The coalescence of their religious and political attitudes was, as the work of Moses demonstrates, vital and strong then, and it remains a force in Jewish life today. It is not suggested they were a typical run-of-the-mill agricultural society: in some ways, they were quite exceptional. Nevertheless, a rehearsal of their familiar characteristics may help a grasp of the essential differences between the pre-civilised and the civilised communities.

It has been necessary to decide the guide-lines of civilisation exactly, for it was alongside civilisation that the social ills really arrived. The key lies in the novel socio-economic structure, which, by its very nature, implied differentials practically unknown to pre-civilised man. There was now a community with gradations and specialisations. Each man had his function. Gone was the all-purpose human of so-called savagery. Role-casting contained the imminent danger of some functions being regarded as superior to others, and, in agricultural societies, distinctions of class and category were quickly evolved. Indeed, in the agriculturally based civilisations of the Ancient World, class distinctions were to be as extreme as mankind has known to the ultimate of slave-owner and slave.

In all the elements hitherto described as characteristic of agrarian life the germs of incohesive society are to be observed. Chief among them must rate the ownership of land and animals. As soon as an individual or family claimed custody of land and the full use of its fruits, then the possibility of more and less was envisaged. The enforced equity of primitive life made the concept of wealth almost irrelevant. In agrarian life the idea of wealth swiftly became a reality, and, in that some had more than others, the social issue of poverty was joined.

One might guess from the closely interlocked character of agricultural life that this upper crust was often composed of the same men playing two or more roles in the social nexus. Consider the logical progression. In a farming society one might expect the leaders to be drawn from the richer land-owners or vice versa. The linkage of political leadership with religious authority must be noted. So, too, might the connection of the priesthood with culture, especially in its verbal aspect. The idea of a landless helot rising from the ranks to the Neolithic equivalent of 10 Downing Street, the Vatican or the Nobel Prize for literature is pleasant but hardly commonsensical. Agriculture produced haves and have-nots on an explicit scale rarely found beforehand. As agriculture became elaborated and its social context more intricate, the distinction became sharper and more precise.

It was in agricultural society that the social problems of poverty, disease, crime and ignorance asserted themselves, simply because they are comparative terms, and comparisons had become inevitable where once they had been difficult and sometimes impossible. The graded and emphatic distinctions between man and man within a common context had the effect of making for judgements of better and worse, and, in the social fields, worse meant poorer, less healthy, more inclined to crime and less well educated.

Whatever the rights and wrongs of a class system (and it could be validly argued that material progress would have been impossible without it) there is no gainsaying the social bonus garnered by the upper class. Poverty—naturally—crime, disease and ignorance have always been the lot of the lower classes, and they have carried a vastly disproportionate burden of social ills. By enjoying and sustaining their wealth, by using it to protect their health, by erecting legal barriers to preserve their rights, and by manipulating educational systems, of whatever kind, in the favour of their offspring, the upper classes have run much less risk of suffering social casualty. It would be ludicrous to pose a class conflict of the healthy, law-abiding, well-educated rich versus the sickly, lawless, illiterate poor, but the balance assuredly leans that way. It was argued previously that social problems are constantly redefined in comparative terms. Part, at least, of this comparing lay in the social distinctions consequent upon the Agricultural Revolution. This has a pseudo-Marxist ring, but it is said without moral or political passion. Poverty, disease, crime and ignorance cannot be provided for until they are identified, and, by polarising the social categories and attitudes, civilisation made the process of identification much simpler.

Poverty, disease, crime and ignorance, nonetheless, were problems and had to be met as such. They underlined the grand irony of civilisation that, in order to prosper, man had to specialise and be unequal and, to that extent, his community lost its cohesion. The very lever that made for progress also undermined. It created the top echelons to experiment and initiate, but, by definition, it created the bottom echelons, and thus friction and instability. Put simply, man gambled a savage, sound society for a civilised, unsound society. The rich, powerful farmers did not, one may suppose, toss and turn in their beds worrying about the poor and enslaved. The critical point was a practical one. What mattered was the point at which poverty, crime, disease or ignorance might tip the delicate balance and destroy the social fabric in which the governing classes lived relatively well.

This could happen in any number of ways. A classic case might have been crop failure, leading to poverty, hence to malnutrition and sickness and possibly epidemic, and thence to disintegration of law and order through crime, small—such as theft—and large—such as rebellion. One should not discount humanitarian and other feelings, but, politically and economically, it may be argued that social provision must most frequently have been made when social ills backlashed at those normally free of them. When the crowd murmured uneasily because of starvation and threatened the peace of the realm, social relief measures might have been called for to appease it. In agrarian societies, where manpower was often the instrument for procuring wealth, there was a vested interest in the well-being of the labour-force, be it slave or free, and this, too, may have led to public relief in harsh times. Again, although better health might have been enjoyed by the rich, the sickness of the labourers must, at some times, have proved improvident to their overlords. Forms of sick relief may have resulted. Another motivation of public health may have been fear. Although the upper crust might have lived in fairer conditions and although the ancients knew little about infection, they must have realised that disease did not discriminate between the wealthy landlord and his servant. This might well have led to public action by way, for instance, of quarantine. It is also conceivable that, if a law or policing device provoked revolt and disorder, the ruling clique might alter it to save their skins. Law became a question of social provision when it provided a socio-judicial frame of reference for all. With education, the labour-force or general citizenry needed to be inducted into those skills which enabled them to operate the socio-economic unit to the advantage of the top people without offering them sufficient skills to threaten the continuity of that unit.

In these and in other cases social problems were probably met by action from above. There might have been agitation from below, but action (save when government was completely overthrown) must have come from above, where the political power and economic resources lay to alleviate distress. And it is suggested that such social provision would normally be proffered when it suited the rulers' book. It is not unthinkable that rulers opened their coffers, provided sick-bays, liberalised the laws and offered educational opportunity, for altruistic reasons, but it is, in all conscience, less likely than that the spur was selfish. There would seem little point in using once obtained power to undermine it; that is, by legislating toward social, economic and judicial equity which could shake the class structure and reduce a community to the classlessness of primitive society. Surely it is more likely that, when and if social provision was made, the providers were counting the benefit to themselves.

One might turn again to the familiar pages of the Old Testament for illustrations of dawning social policy. Famine occurs frequently in the biblical narrative, and, in Genesis 41, Joseph supervised one of the earliest recorded examples of welfare politics. Interpreting Pharaoh's dreams with an aplomb that would have made him the envy of the National Economic Development Council, Joseph persuaded his master to 'take up the fifth part of the land of Egypt in the seven plenteous years'. And when the seven lean years struck, 'Joseph opened all the storehouses and sold unto the Egyptians'. Implicit in such long-term planning was governmental responsibility for the governed. Famine would have proved, in Joseph's own phrase, 'very grievous'. Pharaoh, one might assume, acted out of paternal kindliness towards his people and out of a knowledge that a famished citizenry might prove 'very grievous' to him.

The severe hygienic code of the Hebrew was—and is—a notable feature of Jewish life. One sees the public authority—in this case the priesthood—protecting society by, for instance, placing the leprous individual in quarantine. According to Deuteronomy 23, this sometimes applied generally.

'And thou shalt have a paddle upon thy weapon; and it shall be, when thou wilt ease thyself abroad, thou shalt dig therewith, and shalt turn back and cover that which cometh from thee: For the Lord thy God walketh in the midst of thy camp, to deliver thee, and to give up thine enemies before thee; therefore shall thy camp be holy: that he see no unclean thing in thee, and turn away from thee.'

This recommended exercise in instant sanitation is doubly illuminating. It underlines the strong case for the Jews being among the earliest, perhaps the earliest, public health pioneers, and their social conscience, their guarding of the many against the individual health hazard, is quite remarkable. It also emphasises, in its placing of cleanliness next to godliness, the alignment of government with religion.

This is even more obviously illustrated in legal terms, for the Mosaic law, of which the health regulations formed a part, was represented as a divine pronouncement. The Ten Commandments show this conclusively. And they also show the existence of private property among the pastoral people. The tenth proscribes the coveting of one's neighbour's house, wife, man or maid-servant, ox, ass or, indeed, any of his possessions. Here, and at great length throughout the books of law, social conventions were defined and fully protected by unremitting penalties—'life for life, eye for eye, tooth for tooth, hand for hand, foot for foot, burning for burning, wound for wound, stripe for stripe'. One cannot now judge how faithfully the Hebrews kept their laws, but they had at their disposal an incredibly comprehensive social regulo directing every form of personal relationship.

Looked at from a particular angle, the Pentateuch constitutes a vast, all-pervasive theory of social provision. The criminal, health and property relations of man with his society are there prescribed, and the whole constitutes a body of education which, under the watchful eye of the politico-religious leadership, could be disseminated and controlled. There was poverty, which, during the Israelites' travail in the desert, was met by a divine allotment of quails and manna, while special reductions were allowed, in cases of poverty, in the sacrifices made by cleaned lepers. There was disease, which was treated by a mixture of practical good sense and intricate rituals. There was crime, and this was penalised by tough punishments. The Mosaic law created offences by the hundred, simply by imposing an inflexible myriad of rules upon the Hebrews. There was ignorance in the negative sense that this elaborate life-style was dependent for its sustenance on the didactic transmission of its features to the young. The Israelites, measured against the frame of reference outlined earlier in the chapter, were indubitably civilised. As a facet of that civilisation was the necessity to make provision for social ills.

In this deliberately stylised account of the place of social provision in pre-civilised as opposed to civilised communities, a major principle begins to emerge. It is the degree to which social provision is judged to be expedient in terms of social stability. Given the necessarily 'split' nature of each civilised group, with its haves and have-nots, the former providing and the latter in need of provision, the chief question was how far must we go to sustain the status quo? Too little might, because, for example, of insurrection or famine decimating the labour-force, have been fatal; so might too much in that, by illustration, the 'over-educated' or 'over-paid' have-nots would approximate uncomfortably to haves.

Philosophic, religious, moral and other motives doubtless mattered, and they certainly added a gloss to the style in which social provision schemes were mounted. If one turns to the ancient classical civilisations or to the medieval world, however, the same tenet is apparent. Social provision was, in the main, the spontaneous answer of authorities facing problems likely to undermine social cohesion. These answers adopted the character of the society they served; they could do no other. The angle of the problems altered as the social, economic, cultural and political foundations of communities changed, but they were always the old problems in new guise. And, although there was concurrently a new guise for the answers, the answers, too, were critically obeying the same yardstick of provision for survival.

Chapter 2

Educational and Social Provision in National Communities

Slowly society evolved. Slowly the form of society we recognise as modern came into being, but, however endless the variations of the superstructure, the fundamentals remained constant.

The ancient civilisations had existed around the Mediterranean littoral, ranging in anti-clockwise fashion from Egypt, via the 'Fertile Crescent', watered by the Tigris-Euphrates, and Greece, to Rome. They had been, with one or two notable exceptions, caste-ridden, imperialistic, militaristic and urbanised, and social provision had followed suit. At the time of Christ there were some two million slaves on the Italian peninsula, while many of these communities were embattled camps with highly authoritarian government and teeming urban cores. The Roman policy of *panem et circenses* is the most well-known instance of poor relief, with, at one point, 350,000 of Rome's million population in receipt of daily bounty. Again, Rome is a prime example of the civic need to meet public health hazards in over-crowded conurbations. By the Christian era, Rome had eleven sumptuous public baths and 800 privately-owned pools; there were 1,500 public cisterns and, at one stage, the aqueducts were able to provide a hundred gallons of water per capita—over twice as much as normal consumption today. Similarly, legal and education systems met the requirements of the age, as seen through the eyes of the ruling classes. The judiciary was ever harsh and even brutal, and the schools promoted—take, for example, the case of the Roman school—the instruction of the young in civil or military discipline.

With the collapse of the Roman Empire, however, the pulsations of the ancient world, its heart firmly fixed in the Mediterranean, faded. A new location, in north-west Europe, and a new set of circumstances were to give rise to a novel concept of social provision. For something approaching a thousand years, medieval Europe coped with its political and social problems by reference to diffusion of authority throughout a landed nobility. If it be adopted as a proclivity, rather than as a mechanism, it is fair to see feudalism as the key to that honeycomb of largely self-sufficient agrarian units (in

Edward I's England there were no less than 10,000 manors) in which people eked out their existences. Social provision orientated itself accordingly. Where the ancient turned to city or imperial governance for social care, the medieval relied on his immediate grouping. Man's initial response was to identify with his corporate group, be it manor, guild or order of chivalry, and these determined the nature of his social provision. Many exceptions to this may, given the large tract of time and place involved, be traced, but the characteristic medieval political answer lay in corporate responsibility.

The most familiar example to us may be the Anglo-Saxon rural unit, with its communal responsibility for health, poverty, and—with the folk-moot—law. Even medieval towns exhibited, through the corporateness of the guilds, this underwriting of social casualty for their memberships, given the overall lack of public provision. The castle and the monastery are other illustrations of this mutuality, with groups, joined primarily on a socio-economic base, combining for social protection. At best, the medieval knight was law-giver and social protector; he was (*vide* the Hospitallers) helpmate of the sick; and knighthood, like other medieval corporate mechanisms, was responsible for education for its own perpetuation. The novice knight was trained in the military arts of horsemanship, terrain awareness and combat, with hunting and the tournament of instructional value —all aptly epitomised in that memorable line of poesy: 'there on the 'ill sat 'Arold, on 'is 'orse with 'is 'awk in 'is 'and'. In the Middle Ages, therefore, social provision was most typically organised by personal association, and to be dissociated was to run grave risks of social improvidence.

It is unnecessary to labour the imperceptibility of the change from medieval to modern. No medieval man awoke one morning and declaimed his modernity. Over a longish period, however, basic altera- tions occurred in the major areas of life such as economics, society, the arts, religion and science. These proved critical enough to allow for a retrospective decision that a watershed in European history had taken place. Social provision is geared to its administrative format, and the administrative and political reorganisation within this water- shed involved the erection of nation-states. The slow, ponderous construction of centralised, omnicompetent states gradually led to their replacement of the old-style feudal kingdoms and particularist fragments. The most meaningful feature of this displacement was the passage back of social policy from private into public hands. Nation- hood restated the political ratio of state to individual, and the nature of this ratio was greatly to influence social provision.

Possibly the most important factor was the increasing commercialism of the economy and causes crowded together to accelerate this process. Soon the communal approach of the medieval economy was being replaced by private initiative. Gradually the economy passed from a predominantly *naturalwirtschaft* to a predominantly *geldwirtschaft* or money economy. Neither was ever exclusive, but the emphasis became money rather than land as the key to wealth. A more rational and systematic organisation of money, coinage and banking was a corollary of the growth of capitalism and the fabric of the cash economy was enormously assisted by the inrush of gold from the new world, and, in the three centuries after Columbus's discovery of America, $2\frac{1}{2}$ million kilograms of gold were imported into Europe.

If the order of medievalism came near to vanishing, its restlessness (it was also, after all, a period of strenuous migrant activity) was given rich scope in the discoveries. The opening up of new territories was to prove one of the most important features of commercial expansion. Now north-western Europe became the centre of interest of an enlarged world. Overnight England leapt from being on the edge of a small world to being centrally placed in a bigger one. Thus properly began the expansion of Europe, which, eventually, would contain, by design or precept, every section of the world. The pulsating energy of one continent burst out to dominate the other four continents, and commerce was a major aspect of that domination.

The social changes consequent upon commercialisation were many and varied. The medieval caste system was somewhat broken down, although feudalism was a hardy enough plant to linger in alien soil for many, many years. The duality of a free, landed warrior class and an unfree peasant class tied to the land gradually vanished, but lords and peasants have survived, in one guise or another, to the present time. There was social as well as geographical mobility, but environmental barriers often inhibited change even when legal obstacles had been removed. A rich and a poor, bonded in recognisable hereditary classes, continued, but what was most meaningful sociologically was the upthrust of a third or middle class. The recruitment of this bourgeois or well-to-do class varied according to area and type of economy. Membership has continued to be exceedingly variable, until many sociologists have despaired of identifying the middle class as such. Like the elephant, the middle class is difficult to describe, but its presence is undoubted, and the impossibility of precise definition should not prevent its acceptance. The bourgeoisie are perhaps better delineated in reverse. It would appear that, in any money economy, a group controls the chief elements within that economy, and, by so doing, exacts the premier benefits. In sixteenth-century Spain it was the agriculturally-orientated Hildagos; in Elizabethan England it was a loose compound of squires, landowners and merchants; in nine-teenth-century Europe it was a host of bankers, industrialists, finan-ciers and managers. Certainly no cash economy has yet existed wherein a 'top' grouping of this calibre could not be observed.

In those early days this series of middle class originated among the 10 per cent of the population who were, according to Pirenne, ur-banised and non-agrarian. The leading burghers and merchants and citizens of the towns were in the bourgeois vanguard, their ranks swelled by opportunist peasants and the landless sons of noblemen and, through certain other avenues, both up and down. To these must be added the perennial hangers-on of the bourgeoisie, the professional men such as lawyers, doctors, educators, civil servants and the like. The conjunction of bourgeois with capitalist misleads a trifle, for the control of a money economy is not necessarily to be achieved through private capitalism, nor does it seem possible for a money economy to survive without a controlling faction. The USSR is the most notable example of this today. Seen in this looser frame, the well-to-do classes take on a permanent part in the development of modern Europe. In the more consolidated ethos of later medieval and early modern Europe population continued to expand so that, on the eve of the Industrial Revolution, world population was probably between 700 and 800 million, with a vast concentration of some 80 per cent in Eurasia. Higher population stimulated more trade, and more trade supported more plentiful or more powerful well-to-do classes. An aspect of this combine of population and commercial growth was an increasing size of towns and cities, and it was in this transitory era that the Italian city-states, like Florence or Milan, really came into their own.

This combine of social and economic changes all had one end-result, and that was the disintegration of the medieval corporate group and spirit. Associationism continued to thrive in Europe, but the day of the small in-group was over. The collectiveness of the manor, the order of chivalry, the regular religious order, the gild merchant and the university were inalienably medieval. Whether by choice or no, modern man was thrown back upon himself, and the modern concept of individualism was bred. It was to be some time before individualism reached its zenith, philosophically, in a variety of *laissez-faire* dogmas and, economically, in the cut-throat competition of industrialism. But man as a creature freed from the social restraints of the Middle Ages had made his bow by 1500. It would be over-sentimental to ascribe all this to a change in man's consciousness, for it must be emphasised that individualism was a reaction to circumstance.

It has been suggested that medievalism was polarised in nature and that there had been the minute and gigantic (for instance, the 'universalism' of the Catholic Church or the Latin culture over against the introversion of the monastery or the local ascendancy, say, of a tribal or regional dialect) but rarely the mean. The move to modernity was often a reversal to the norm and the rough equalising of the two extremes. Man's medieval context was the huge canvas of Christian universalism and the tiny shelter of his association, be it manor or gild. His modern context was the state, and, in its very formulation, each state both cut a chunk out of Christendom and compounded bits of particularism. This engendered an erasure of the groups and corporations, and permitted their smooth inclusion within statehood. The initial loyalty of a man to his manor, his lord, his abbey or his gild was replaced by a national identification. This, then, was another angle on individualism. The group was enlarged; each man was a member of a sizeable corporate body, namely, the state. It was large enough for the bond to be impersonal and abstract, and it was this lack of intimacy which helped throw individualism into a starker light. In this sense, then, individualism was a trifle specious; it was merely membership of a large communality, but this did not obstruct, rather did it stimulate, the practice of private enterprise. His inclusion within a numerically high and qualitatively complex group increased the permutations of opportunity beyond count, and the freedom to soar within this spacious cage was indeed individualistic when set against the cabined pens of medieval existence. The rich, healthy and well-educated individuals tended to rise to form the top layer of the new society, leaving the poor, sick and lawless individuals floundering beneath. The desolate, wandering vagrant personified the social degradation of early modern times.

These radical alterations were occurring within the pale of the state. The state was the economic unit, and the upper and lower and middle classes existed as segments of the nation. In the medieval period social status had been much more cross-sectional, with serfdom, the landed nobility and even the great financial families, like the Fuggers, living opposed to custom, which had been so necessary among agrarian and operating at an international level. Now authority was back in public hands, and, if poor relief was to be offered, the state could determine the terms. Similarly with health. The state could now dictate regulations, such as quarantine and vermin control; health could now become 'public' where once it had been, at best, the responsibility of municipal authorities, and, more usually, left to chance. In the legal sphere, the change was most complete. Although, in effect, many crimes were committed against individuals, they were, in law, committed against the state. The state was, and is, but a conglomeration of individuals, and the national legal system became their protection. A series of national legal codes developed, and their emphasis was on rationality, an essential for trading communities, as opposed to custom, which had been so necessary among agrarian groups. It was now also possible to bring education within national sway, indeed, to use it for the express purpose of indoctrinating the young in the tenets of the state's political doctrines and religious beliefs, as well as schooling them vocationally in the skills necessary for the sustenance of the economy. Thus, across post-medieval Europe—and the world—the concept of nationally overseen education systems has been widely practised.

There was, appropriately and without coincidence, the Scientific Revolution at hand to assist commercialism and its adjunct, colonialism. Compasses and telescopes helped traders and colonists to make their way overseas, and guns enabled them to establish their beachheads. It is scarcely too much of a simplification to argue that Europeanisation would not have been possible without firepower. More peacefully, builders and surveyors and shipwrights were busily making their crafts more efficient. Within the framework of scientific method, the old hit-or-miss style of empiricism gave way to a much more rational and much less chancy practice, which affected agricultural as well as manufacturing and transporting operations. Technological advance was also to make its mark in administrative circles, not only by beginning and then easing the task of large-scale literary communication, but by establishing all manner of rational mechanisms in the corridors of power. The Scientific Revolution was to place at man's behest the technical and administrative potential for resolving problems of social evils. It was, and is, in the power of science to provide for the poor and cure the sick, and to make available such bounty on a worldwide basis.

It was not surprising that the critical changes occurring in economics, society and science should be paralleled with similar reorientations of culture and religion. The cultural revolution was, in a word, the Renaissance. In terms of overall perspective, this cultural upheaval had two important historical effects, appertaining to individualism and to statehood or nationalism. Nationalism was and remains the political counterweight to individualism, and the Renaissance provided psychological and cultural provender for both.

The same recrudescence of individualist spirit and national awareness was discernible in the Reformation. The political import of the
Reformation lies in the growth of national churches. Religion was
obviously a more potent and fiery political force than in later years,
and any form of political organisation had to take note of it. The
unification of areas into nation-states involved a recognition of this
force, and, in more or less degree, states moved to obtain some
authority over the national church. Some of them, such as England,
demonstrated their internal unity by a complete abrogation of the
external and international bondage of Catholicism, and where
countries remained Roman Catholic, their monarchs often negotiated
styles of internal control. Most compelling of all, the nation-states,
whatever the credo at stake, insisted on a harsh measure of conformity.
In their infancy, emergent states were careful of their stability, and
religious tolerance could mean political insecurity and suicide.

Perhaps the bourgeoisie grasped, possibly subconsciously, at the
Protestant beliefs, as at nationalist ones, as a mental support for its
economic creed. Protestantism seemed to free acquisitive economics
from the traditional ethics which had held competitiveness in check.
The coincidence of the Protestant religion and capitalism was perhaps
that of an intermediary stage between complete submission to the
church and its complete eschewal. Protestantism served to shepherd
capitalism from the static past to the dynamic future. Max Weber has
argued that the capitalist spirit was 'the crucial agent' in the economic
transformation, and that the Reformation justified work as the 'fulfilment of a God-given task'.

The Renaissance and the Reformation were not the only intellectual challenges at the threshold of modernism. Political philosophy
was adjusting to modern demands, and the Christocentric views of
St Augustine and St Thomas Aquinas and the discussion of empire
and papacy were giving way to a more thoroughgoing theory of state.
The philosophy of statecraft and the blueprint for establishing and
maintaining the state were announced in uncompromising and un-
ambiguous phrases by that much maligned political scientist, Niccolo
Machiavelli. He was the first notable commentator to examine politics
within the ambit of the state. Here began the lengthy tradition of state
theory, and many were shocked by Machiavelli's lean, tough attitude
towards the need for the new-style prince to be ruthless and effective.
It is important to stress the ideal of the efficient state, for it was very
much to mould new attitudes of social welfare, social justice and
social administration.

Each state, firstly, was a conglomeration of particularist fragments and, at the same time, a hardening of borders within the European community at large. A mild romanticism has led to a belief in spontaneous combustion as the formative force in nationalism. There were nationalist movements, but they were rarely successful alone, as opposed to when they became the instrument of *realpolitik*. In reality, each nation was not so much a unification as an expansion of its central core. For instance, German unification was, in effect, the extension of Prussia, just as Italian unification was tantamount to an extension of Piedmont-Sardinia.

The system of administration, as well as its nature, was to be ruled by the dictates of the national core. A simple example was the odd geographical location of some capital cities, such as London, Madrid, Berlin, St Petersburg and later Moscow. They were well-placed to administer the core, but not necessarily the whole, and this, too, was to affect policy implementation.

A second common denominator was the creation of nation-states under the aegis of an autocratic royal house, normally associated with the metropolitan region of the new state. Medievalism's attachment to kingship thus evolved its own destroyer, for these new-type monarchies grew from the feudal kingdoms of the Middle Ages. The English royal house was quick to establish a dominance which eventually reached its apogee in the Tudor reigns, while the hard grafting of the Capetian kings in France prepared the ground for the glories of the Bourbons. These were absolute monarchies, and they were of a different order from the older feudal kingdoms, where authority swayed to and fro according to the deployment of feudal forces.

The erection of centralised administrations was to be of the utmost importance for social policy. The existence of a state and a state policy was of no avail without an effective administrative format. The Tudor Administrative Revolution, as G. R. Elton, its eloquent recorder, has entitled it, was the British reflection of this. In the 1530s particularly, a central, public bureaucracy was gradually established. Through Parliament and through the local magistracies, the state enacted its commands and attempted to see them fulfilled.

The main ingredients of these new regimes were threefold. True to the changing economic character of the times, they were squarely founded on financial sufficiency. The new kings were political supremos, not landed noblemen, and tried to put themselves and their realms on a healthy fiscal footing. Francis Bacon, far-sighted and acute adviser to the Tudors, claimed that no state 'would prospere or be worshipful undere a poore kynge'. Another essential instrument was well-disciplined armed forces, and the military sign of modernity was the substitution of standing, often mercenary, armies for the feudal levy with its equestrian leadership. A class of administrators makes up this trio of prerequisites for state management. These were necessary not only to man the central bureau but also the local agencies of the state. A good example is the English justice of the peace, the country squire ready to ensure, if in a somewhat amateurish fashion, that the Tudor writs ran properly in his locality.

Finance, defence and bureaucracy thus swiftly engaged the thoughts of modern statesmen and monarchs, and, equally quickly, the three reverberated one upon the other, with bureaucrats collecting money to pay for soldiery as an oversimplified instance of this. Because of the way in which states were fashioned, because of the mood in which this shaping occurred and because of the abrasive relations of state and state and, frequently, state and citizen, this triple obsession was to remain. Inevitably, the priority accorded these items has operated to the detriment of social welfare in the nation-states, where it has normally been relegated to the secondary or tertiary grades of governmental consideration.

Absolute monarchy and the extension of a central core were two common themes in the creation of European statehood, and alliance of the monarchy with the well-to-do was a third. The king and his middle-class subjects normally needed one another, especially in the earlier phases of national development. They were locked in contest against the same enemy, that is those who had a vested interest in the perpetuation of particularism. Overseas the military and political protection of the monarchy was invaluable, as a hundred colonial skirmishes and quarrels will testify. Domestic stability and colonial expansion were the kingly concessions most desired by the bourgeoisie. In return the well-to-do or bourgeoisie gave faithful support to the monarchy. They provided the services performed during feudal times by the landed nobility. They gave advice and counsel in the national assemblies that sprang up—notably the English Parliament, the French states-general and the German Bundesrat—they sent recruits to the civil service, they rendered valuable service in local administration, they helped to dispense justice and, most important of all, they provided money. They were the main beneficiaries of a money economy; the governance of a money economy needed substantial funds, and, in chief, the middle classes, of whatever complexion, supplied them.

The effect of this entente on social provision was far-reaching. Transition to statehood and the *geldwirtschaft* dislocated traditions wholesale. The communal and charitable attitudes of medieval times were disturbed. At a time when social provision was more necessary, or, at best, requiring changed responses, the fulcrum of economic and political power was shifting towards a class which, in general, thought along lines of independence and self-help. Sometimes expediency might dictate welfare enactments, while the other side of the medallion—humanism and benevolence—must not be discounted. But the classic victims of social ills were always the lower orders, and their relation to their superiors was to alter. The mutually acceptable balance of the land-tie between lord and serf was lost in the dynamism of modern life. The majority found that social problems and their treatments had taken a different twist. Whether they were better or worse is not, at this point, the concern—what matters is the difference introduced into social policy through the increase in authority of the commercially based middle classes.

Having accepted all the many reservations of this definition of a watershed, one can see 1500 as a pivotal date, as a time by which the balance had fallen in favour of modernity. The historical unit of nation-state plus money economy, what Toynbee has called 'the pagan deification' of territorial and commercial slabs, has not yet been altered. There have been modifications, but industrialism is a projection of commercialism and political changes have all taken place within the ambit of the state, essentially in the completion of middle-class authority at the expense of monarchy.

However unduly simplified this analysis may appear, it is accurate enough for the purpose of investigating social administration. In its European manifestation, social provision comes in only two packages, non-state and state. This is not to suggest that either brand was remarkable for the quality of its social provision, but that the decision as to whether or of what kind it should be lay there. It is because social policy has been state policy since the first signs of the close of the medieval era, that it has been necessary to examine the origins of the state at some length.

This new commercial nationalism wholly altered the slant of social problems. The production of goods was undoubtedly stepped up, but the even tenor of medieval distribution was lost. The producer and distributor controlled consumption under the aegis of the state, and the active and productive accordingly benefited. Neither merchant nor prince had much time for the socially inadequate, for the sick, the aged, the thriftless, the ignorant or the misfits. The state was not only the town but the castle writ large, and the improvident or ineffective could be forced to the wall as in a medieval siege. Often this bore no relation to production, and there could be pockets of want amidst affluence. Money had almost replaced land as the key to livelihood, and unemployment began to replace famine as the chief cause of poverty. The disintegration of the familiar agrarian routines promoted mobility of an unprecedented style and scale.

The most typical and the most comprehensive social problem facing early modern Europe was, therefore, vagrancy. The towns and cities drew them like iron filings to a magnet, and urban squatting combined with rural perambulation to form a broadly sweeping social menace. It constituted an interlocking threat to the state in all social fields. There was pauperdom, with its attendant sapping at national morale and resources, and, because of its mobility, difficult to manage; there was ill-health caused by impoverishment and menacing to the community because of the creation of squalid conditions and the haphazard movement of the sick poor; there was disorder at all levels, from poaching and minor theft in the country to grave rioting in the towns; there was a kind of vocational-cum-social illiteracy of people unfitted for any role in a new form of society.

In brief, modern social structure went near to reversing pre-civilised social concepts. During the phase of predatory tribalism, the communalistic element was strong enough to limit the inequalities between richest and poorest, to define crime very much in community terms, and, together with the rigours of prehistoric existence, even managed to reduce the difficulty of ill-health to a communal level. During medieval times a kind of half-way stage had been reached. Agrarian group life allowed for a certain amount of corporate activity, with crime basically an offence against the group, poverty often suffered by most members of a group and disease frequently attacking the whole group. In the modern age, the individual element, on balance, came to the fore. The individual was poor, and fundamentally had no devices other than his own to aid him, or he was, equally through his own actions, rich. According to his economic station the individual was more or less able to cater for his own health needs by purchasing private medical attention, a healthier habitat and items like fresher water and more wholesome food. As medicine and building and other aspects of the social environment improved, this gap widened. In more primitive times, for instance, if a cure for some complaint had not been discovered, riches were of no avail. When, in an individualist situation, a cure was obtainable, it became marketable to those able to afford it. Crime became much more an affront to the individual's privacy and personal property, and less a question of breaking caste conventions. Ignorance became, more and more, a denial of the skills necessary for fruitful membership of the national elite. Against this European background, England was perhaps the first state actually to move towards a national policy, and this serves as a suitable example.

The technical achievement of the agrarian and commercial revolutions of the sixteenth century were unhappily marred by social dislocation, and Tudor governments were rightly concerned. With some justification they regarded destitution as a threat to peace, and they had grave misgivings about the undermining of social stability. They lent an ear to public opinion which fully blamed enclosures for social problems, rather than seeing them as a symptom of a general dislocation—'horn and thorn shall make England forlorn' ran the doggerel. They believed that corn would run into short supply and that taxation would drop, and that the shire levies would disintegrate to the detriment of the nation's defence. 'We do reken', wrote one doleful critic, 'that shepherds be but yll archers.'

The Tudor response was a somewhat vain and ineffective swiping at the new market and other economic forces, with a large number of state enactments. Amidst this welter of state action there arose the Tudor Poor Law to meet the requirements of the new poor, who were thrown up by all the uncertainties of a national money economy. At first there was a haphazard mix-up of charity and savagery on a most inconsistent pattern, pleasingly summarised in the nursery rhyme 'Hark, Hark, the Dogs Do Bark, the Beggars Have Come to Town'. The City of London, faced with the largest problem of poverty and sickness led the way. In 1547 it arranged for England's first direct taxation for social welfare, taxes which were 'a little grutched and repined', but it was a start. From the end of the sixteenth to the middle of the seventeenth century, the poor law grew more systematic in its national administration. The conditions of the lower orders were probably worsening, but the capacity of the centralised bureaucracy was growing. Statutes required the appointment of Overseers of the Poor in every parish to levy poor rates, provide for the destitute and punish transgressors, under the general guidance of the magistrates. This straightforward clarification of the system was a direct statement of civil power, and it was supported by the profoundly important activities of the Privy Council.

Education, too, came under the thrall of the state, with apprenticeship—'the Englishman's school' as G. O. Trevelyan called it—governed by such legislation as the Statute of Artificers in 1563. The grammar school—and in the sixteenth century no boy lived more than twelve miles from one—met the commercial and administrative demands of the Tudor state, as succinctly expressed in Thomas Elyot's

The Governor. Both institutions were concerned with social discipline and religious and political conformity—there were supposedly compulsory elements of this kind in the syllabus and teachers had to swear the Schoolmaster's Oath, vowing allegiance to the Queen and her supremacy in church affairs. Education was regarded as one way of 'winning the west for Protestantism'.

The Privy Council also had oversight of the repression of civil outrage and crime. This was accomplished through the medium of the justices of the peace and the work of the parish constables. All in all, the central government through the Privy Council attacked poor relief, health, law and order and schooling at base, and they adopted the existing local agency of the parish as the ambit for these kinds of social provision. Indeed, once established, this bipartite structure of English administration was to survive to the present day, and must be regarded as an important element in any reappraisal of today's situation.

Thus the pattern of social provision in England, as in other nation-states, was formulated, corresponding, in character, to the dictates of the money economy and its dominant well-to-do. But, although the fashion of social administration changed with the alteration in the political and economic fabric, the underlying theme persisted. Social expediency remained the golden rule. Education operated, like other forms of social provision, in so far as it sustained the state and in so far as it prevented the state from social collapse. So persistent indeed is this theme that, in any attempt to reform the social system, it must be considered with the utmost weight.

Chapter 3

The Centralist Approach to Social and Educational Provision

The nation-state and the money economy became the stage for society's performance, not only in the West, but on a paramountly world wide basis. This was an important feature of that 'Europeanisation' which now affects practically every corner of our planet. It is not just the actual colonisation of various areas, and the heavy metropolitan residue which remains in the aftermath of decolonisation. Nor is it even that cultural or diplomatic colonisation which, either with its Americanised or Russianised tinge, affects almost all tracts of the earth's surface. From the viewpoint of social administration, the more meaningful elements concern the all but complete tendency of communities to formulate a *geldwirtschaft* within the pale of nationhood.

There have, of course, been major modifications within this politico-economic arena. Probably the most compelling have been the intense introduction of industrial technology into the commercial nexus and the proclivity towards some form of oligarchic or parliamentary government. The former has, self-evidently, changed the whole character and quantity of commercial transactions, and, with manifestations like multinational companies and international trading compacts, such as the Common Market, national boundaries seem to be sundered. Nonetheless, the basis of decision about such activities remains firmly in the state. As for the latter, the move towards some type of parliamentary or shared governance, it came as a result of the eventual disintegration of the political contract engineered between the absolute monarchies and their well-to-do or bourgeois supports. These, in simple terms, began to need monarchical oversight less and less, as, alternatively, kingship needed more and more support. Thus over a long phase, stretching from our own Civil War period of the seventeenth century to well into the present era, this process has been enjoined. Now all over Europe, and much of the world, national existences are more or less controlled by politico-managerial factions. These range considerably over a gamut of typologies, with some (to right and left, politically speaking) apparently less subservient to any form of public will than others. This means that, for instance, the government of the USSR seems, superficially, to vary widely from that of the USA because of different attitudes to political debate and economic organisation, arising from their respective geographies and traditions. But, taking a longer view, it is likely that, a thousand years hence, the future historian will see more clearly the similarities of two huge, federalised states, with cash economies and a centrally controlled government, and of a membership and approach differing in degree rather than kind.

To put it negatively, no major nation-state has a valid, thorough-going system of communal or popular control. Our own political system, often used as a splendid model and certainly offering viable channels for public concern and pressure, is 'parliamentary' rather than 'popular'. Put another way, we enjoy 'representative' government, and there have been many important advantages and reasons for the evolution of such a system; but it is not 'popular' or 'democratic' government from the angle of people having a close, day-by-day influence and watch on their community's activities, social, political or economic. As Rousseau reminded us, the English have democracy once every five years on General Election day; throw in the local government elections, and his point is well-taken.

Turning to the more social aspects concomitant with these political and economic modifications of the 'national cash-nexus' society, these may be fairly summarised by the phenomenon of what Herman Finer strikingly called 'congregation'. This has been the process whereby more and more people have herded together in less and less space for both life and livelihood. The phenomenon embraces an interactive threesome of obvious enough components which may be designated as population, urbanisation and industrialisation. The statistics and subsequent problems of the demographic explosion need little further rehearsal. The population of the world has been, it will be recalled, estimated at between 5 and 10 million about 10,000 BC on the eve of the agricultural revolution. In AD 1500, with Europe, at least, poised to break fully into the process of statehood and commerce, it has been calculated that the world housed some 500 million. Now it approaches 4,000 million, and AD 2000, some claim, will see even this alarming figure almost doubled to some 7,500 million. In 1960 two-thirds of the world's population lived on and from the land, whereas, by the end of the century, it will be only one-third, with as many as 5,000 million living in towns and cities. For instance, between now and 1985 Bandung's populace will expand by 242 per cent while already there are twelve of the world's cities with populations of 7 million or more. Industrial production presents an equally straightforward case of rapid expansion. Using the world's industrial production of 1953 as the norm of 100, it had risen, by 1970, to approaching 200, whereas it had been only 5 in 1870. Electricity is expected to increase by 300 per cent or 400ˉ per cent over the next twenty years, while that standard substance of man's industrial activity—iron ore—is now consumed at four times the rate of 1950, which incidentally, and save for other developments, would mean its exhaustion by 2050 AD.

Turning parochially to the United Kingdom, one can remark the early, miniature version of this global process. The population of England and Wales rose from $5\frac{1}{2}$ million in 1700 to 13 million in 1831, and on to 29 million by the turn of the century. The prevalence of this demographic explosion in towns can be noted as easily. In the first fifty years of the last century, the country's population doubled, but Blackburn had, in the same time, a 500 per cent increase from 13,000 to 65,000, and Bradford sprang from 13,000 to a colossal 104,000—an incredible eight-times increase. Urbanisation had arrived: Blackburn and Bradford were the Jakarta, Lagos and Karachi of the day. Industrialism was moving as quickly, with Manchester boasting fifty-two mills in 1802 where, twenty years previously, there had only been a couple. Spun cotton figures jumped from $1\frac{1}{4}$ million pounds in 1741 to 22 million pounds just forty-six years later. By 1900 only 9 per cent of the active population of Great Britain were working in agriculture.

In 1066 the population was 1.5 million. Today it stands, for the United Kingdom, at about 55 million. And 80 to 90 per cent of our children in school are urban children. These urban-dwellers live in and off a highly complex industrialised economy, and they are packed into only one-eighth of the land area—a fitting illustration of the confining character of urbanism. The United Kingdom remains the twelfth most populous country in the world and almost half its gross national product is in the form of industrial production with, in 1971, £9,000 million of exports and nearly £10,000 million of imports. England, it should perhaps not wish to boast, led the world in 'congregation'.

Just as each move in political evolution—pre-civilised to civilised, medieval to early modern—changed the slant of the age-old social problems that forever confront mankind, so did these principal modifications or projections of the national economy likewise alter the character of social ills. Congregation brought a character to the four corners of social disadvantage with which we have primarily been concerned. Larger populations, cramped in larger towns and confined in larger factories, soon writ large the social problems of society. Poverty was not now the vagrant group nor the occasional beggar nor the once-in-a-while destitute family; it became the entire community underemployed and the entire factory thrown out of work. When, for example, the Cotton Famine of the 1860s or the Great Depression of the 1930s occurred, the sporadic practice of parochial relief was at a discount. Ill-health was not now the stricken family nor even village; it became the entire community subject to the risk of epidemic. When, for example, cholera afflicted the large cities of Britain with its abrasive terror, quarantine and the old style infirmaries were futile counters. Crime was not now the sneak-thief nor the aggressive malcontent on farm or in hamlet; it became the plethora of 'depredations' (as the Victorians termed them) lost in the anonymity of the new conurbations, alongside the dangers of mass disorder resulting from economic and political disputes. When, for example, railway and canal robberies vied with massive prostitution and violent strikes as the chief dislocations of public order, the 'know-everyone' and the haphazard watch systems, and even the use of the military, became redundant. Ignorance was not now the apprentice in need of a trade or a credo by which to live nor a few children preparing for jobs requiring a grasp of elementary letters or accounts; it became thousands of urbanised children needful of literacy to fit them for the more elaborate techniques of an industrialised economy. When, for example, by the 1860s, there were, in several large towns, thousands of illiterate children with neither work-places nor schools to attend, a spasmodic offering of dames' schools, charity schools and Sunday schools barely formed any kind of answer.

To pursue the educational point a little further, it is important to realise exactly why a public system of schooling was inaugurated. The debate tended to circle around the use of literacy, and whether, once schooled, the populace would improve itself by a perusal of the Holy Bible and other standard tracts on British moral practice, or sink under a debilitating scrutiny of scabrous, revolutionary rags. Would Bernard de Mandeville's shepherds and farmworkers be inhibited by knowledge from labouring on regardless with cheerfulness and equanimity, or was Lord John Russell correct to draw attention to the argument that 'by combining moral teaching with general instruction the young may be saved from the temptations to crime'?

The balance of the argument was, however, probably turned in favour of public literacy by the weight of vocational and civic necessity. It was an evermore complicated economy, and the adult workman, able to read instructions, or the adult clerk, ready to pen

invoices, was in demand. Similarly, the civic structure of an industrialised, urbanised nation-state might totter unless its citizenry
was literate enough to be summoned here and ordered there by post.
When scarcely any of Liverpool's twenty-two thousand cellar-dwellers
could read the eviction orders delivered to them in the 1840s, it was
quite a forceful argument for compulsory courses in 'officialese' for
all. The conformity of reading became and remains as integral a prerequisite for the maintenance of the modern nation as conformity of
religious belief for the sustenance of the early modern nation. One
must never forget why the Victorians—and their counterparts abroad
—embarked on their national education ventures. Although more
purely educational principles, both academic and humane, were by no
means disallowed, the economic and administrative pointers counted
for most. Nor is the theme quiescent. In 1870 W. E. Forster, introducing the 1870 Education Act, claimed that

> 'upon the speedy provision of elementary education depends our
> industrial prosperity . . . Civilised communities throughout the
> world are massing themselves together, each mass being measured
> by its force; and if we are to hold our position among men of our
> own race or among the nations of the world, we must make up the
> smallness of our numbers by increasing the intellectual force of the
> individual.'

Just short of a hundred years on, in 1963, the Robbins Report on
Higher Education could not 'believe that modern societies can achieve
their aims of economic growth and higher cultural standards without
making the most of the talents of their citizens. This is obviously
necessary if we are to compete with other highly developed countries
in an era of rapid technological and social advance' The tune changes,
but the melody lingers on.

The significant characteristic of social expediency thus recurs and
not only apropos education. Once more it was the middle class or well-
to-do who were, eventually, threatened by the new format of social
distress. The most acutely heard argument for a reformed distribution
of poor relief in the 1830s was the extravagance of the old ways, for
charitable alms and parish rates were messy and expensive, so it
seemed, responses to the new-style poverty. In any event, the unrest,
economic, social and political, which accompanied the massive temporary impoverishment of the cyclic trading depression constituted
another kind of threat to the employing classes and their professional
associates. This may be linked with the fear of dislocation caused by a
rate of theft and by mass disorder in the confined purlieus of the

towns. The local squire, safe from the footpad behind the walls of his rural homestead and with his loyal retainers in constant support, had become the shopkeeper or mill-owner, his property and resources at risk constantly to theft or assault. As for health, these same over-crowded environs raised the hazard of disease for the industrialised, urbanised middle classes. The sanitary and the allied water supply problems of mid-nineteenth century gradually assaulted the physical well-being and senses of the middle classes almost as much as those of the working classes, while cholera steadfastly refused to distinguish between master and labourer.

There was, obviously, no attempt to offer an across-the-board pro-tection for the citizen against social evils. There was no suggestion that the millhand had as much right to or, for that matter, need of the wealth, health and learning of the millowner. It was, at best, an attempt to preserve a balance, whereby the funds expended on poor relief or public health or law and order insured society against col-lapse. It was, usually, an attempt to allow the minimal public support which would avoid ruination and sustain the status quo. The Vic-torians were most honest about this, for they constantly referred the effectiveness or otherwise of social provision to its effect on the gross national product. An idle or unemployed populace, living extrava-gantly off the rates, the loss of work caused by unnecessary illness and premature death, the expense of an inefficient policing system at a time of rising theft, the adverse influence on trade of clogged streets and noisome surrounds, the inability of an ill-educated workforce to compete competently in the growing world labour mart—these were the kind of causes which spurred them to reform. The human and economic waste startled.and disgusted them into a huge enthusiasm for social reformation.

It might be argued that this element of social expediency had and has a threefold character. First, there must be necessity, more or less pressing, in national terms. Only occasionally has a government em-barked, say, on a piece of educational or welfare legislation unless the need was a compelling one; that is, the case has been overwhelmingly social rather than moral. For example, in education, the argument for raising the school leaving age over the last eighty years has critically been couched in terms of the requirements—quality and quantity—of the labour market. Second, there must be availability, on a wide enough scale to meet this degree of necessity; there must, in fact, be some wherewithal at hand to implement such decisions. In education, for example, this had two sides. The economy had to be in a position to release children for schooling and still operate successfully; in other words, the reverse of 'necessity'. The other, perhaps, more important, side was financial. The economy had to be able to afford educational development. Education—like welfare and health and even law and order—lay in the margin of economic activity. If there were resources available, they could be so utilised. Indeed, it has been convincingly suggested that, rather than more education producing high technology economies, it is high technology economies that can afford the luxury of more education. Third, there must be viability. Unless an administrative format existed to put whatever schemes were chosen into action, then little could be achieved. This is a point sometimes neglected, but until, for instance, telephones, typewriters, duplicators and the other bagatelle of bureaucratic existence—as well as the very bureaucratic machinery itself—were available, it was not possible to organise an education—or a health or an insurance—service on a national scale.

The style of this viable administrative formula has had enormous repercussions. It is instructive to note the similarity of administrative approach in the United Kingdom to these four major social problems with which this survey is presently concerned. The early response of urbanised society to the 'mass' impact of social ills was based on the 'preventive principle'. It was an outcrop of Benthamism and the idea of the freeplay of individuals leading to a sum total of the greatest happiness for the greater number. Such were the inhibitions placed on this process by ignorance, idleness, ill-health and illegality that men were not free to liberate their spontaneous impulses towards the good of the commonwealth. There thus grew the 'tutelary' concept of the state, commonly associated with Edwin Chadwick, whereby the state would act to clear the arena for this free and liberal activity. It was, theoretically, the state tutoring its clientele towards freedom, legislating, as it were, for *laissez-faire*. Hence the 'less eligibility' principle, started in the new poor law with the Workhouse Test, was an attempt to force as many people as possible on to the labour mart by making the relief system more unpleasant than the most menial and lowly work. The 'preventive' police system was an effort to make crime 'less eligible' than steadfast and lawful endeavour by ensuring as complete a constabulary cover as was needed to exclude theft. The 'preventive' public health system, with those twin components of water supply and sanitary outlet, tried to avoid disease by removing its sources. Early educational activity—grants-in-aid for denominational schools and later the School Board movement—were attempts to encourage local and church and other non-state agencies to offer an educational chance to as wide a public as possible, with a more complex civic and vocational pattern guaranteeing that illiteracy was socially and economically 'less eligible' than literacy.

The administrative 'tutelle', as it has been called, of the middle decades of the last century was justified in this negative manner, along the lines of creating an 'artificial harmony of interests'. Other motives and explanations abounded, but this one was a common denominator: it gave an often blurred but firmly constant justification for the Victorians' highly expedient and highly practical concern with social reform. In organisational terms there followed from this any number of similarities. In each case there was an executive dichotomy evolved between an increasingly powerful central body and some form of local committee or board, normatively with an elective element. There was, for instance, Board (later Ministry) of Health: local Board of Health (later municipal Health Committee); Poor Law Commission (later Board): local Board of Guardians; Home Office: Watch Committee; Board (later Ministry, later Department) of Education: School Board (later Education Committee). These dichotomies were very much shaped by the Benthamite view of the strong central core and the intention locally to identify governed and governor as close as possible.

Within this structure, another series of administrative methods was developed. There was the concentration on the qualified and trained professional—doctor, nurse, sanitary engineer, health visitor, welfare and social worker, policeman, teacher and so forth. There was cost-accounting (Robert Lowe's 'payment by results' is the most, but not the only, notorious educational illustration) and there was, from school and factory to health and police, a vast inspectoral network. More and more of the training for these groups became intramural, that is, negotiated in colleges and so on, and, with the growth of prescribed qualifications and examinations, the professional exclusiveness and mystiques also grew. This had many advantages over the previous frighteningly haphazard arrangements, but it carried with it certain hazards at the same time; for instance, a sequence of divorcements of professionals from laities.

A further fascinating congruence is to be found in the institutional character of the new administrative frame. Its rationale was mainly industrial with military adjuncts. The novel economic institution was the factory: this was the economic version of 'concentration'. Sometimes consciously, sometimes unconsciously, the Victorians turned to the mill and the mine for their answer. Faced with social ills *en masse,* the 'factory formula' was their sustained response. Up rose the gaunt workhouse to combat poverty, the huge hospital (often a projection of the poor law) to grapple with disease, the large prison to meet rising crime, and the massive school to deal with illiteracy. Obviously, smaller versions—the old poorhouse, charity hospitals, bridewells and dames' schools—had existed. What was innovative was the development of a network of these heavyweight institutions across the country. The schools were, it was claimed, the 'steam-power principle applied to the intellect'. There was a strong military flavour. The prison service, many hallmarks of the police system, certain aspects of hospital discipline and much, over the last hundred and fifty years, of the education system have been quite regimental. Alongside this, workhouse master, prison governor, hospital matron and head teacher corresponded to the works manager; assistant overseer with dormitory, warder with wing, sister with ward and teacher with classroom corresponded to foreman with workshop. The division of labour and the split functions of industry were mirrored in the segregation of the workhouse, the prison and the hospital into particular categories of inmate, while the streaming by 'age, aptitude and ability' of our schools completes the picture of orderly classification. Part-barrack, part-factory, these agencies created a tight principle of incarceration as the main Victorian response to social troubles. Incarceration: paupers, patients, prisoners and pupils were all herded into ever vaster conglomerates.

Once under way, the administrative impetus led inexorably towards heftier central control. In strong waves state control increased, with the post-1870 era, the pre-1914 era and the post-1945 era showing the chief emphases, until, in our own times, the level of state interference is very high. Certainly the previous dichotomous central/local balance seems to be weighed much more towards the former, and the prison, health, education and social service organisations demonstrate substantial measures of central authority. It should be added that, since the formation of the nation-state and its administrative resolution in the sixteenth century, centralisation has probably been moving on apace, despite some apparent setbacks to its onward march. One aspect of this is the astronomical mathematics of public finance, with the exchequer handling millions of pounds of income from various forms of taxation on a scale which dismays many a modern citizen and would have completely staggered the Victorian. Add to the social services the other undertakings under central control, from the traditional state's roles of defence and foreign policy to the newer economic functions of the state *vis-à-vis* transport, energy, housing and so on.

The state controls a considerable amount of the individual's life-style, and a substantial allotment from the gross national product is under the thrall of the central authority. The Welfare State is the pivot of this high degree of state interference, with the National Health Service at the hub of an extensive life-support system for every individual from cradle to grave. With so much of industry and communications either directly or indirectly under state control, from post office to steel-works, from BBC to NCB, there is no gainsaying the lengths to which the state's authority runs. It is also fair to argue that the local government agencies have lost some of their potency, as national standards, centralised action and heavy national finance have grown in number and import.

Not that this is a peculiarly British phenomenon. It is so marked a process throughout the West and much of the remainder of the world that it might almost be seen as a natural and automatic stage in the life of a national money economy. It is interesting to trace the development towards a common end of countries which superficially seem to have variable beginnings. One illustration of this lies in the philosophic basis of differing nations. The *laissez-faire* doctrines of Victorian England suggested a violent reaction against state intervention, especially with the operation of free trade in the commercial sector. This passed from the 'natural' to the 'artificial' view of the liberated state, with the state in its 'tutelle' capacity. This, in turn, acted as a bridge to the long haul of 'collectivism', with the public rather than the private sector in the ascendant. In the United States Jefferson spoke of an 'agrarian democracy', with 'frugal government' and neighbours so far apart, as he picturesquely said, that they could not hear one another's dogs bark. Both the commercial pressures, represented by Alexander Hamilton, and the need to combat them, represented by Andrew Jackson, required and won a strong federal response. This slowly evolved through the New Deal and wartime legislation toward a vast federal mechanism responsible for the funding and oversight of huge programmes of internal and external aid, defence, space probes and so forth. The early socialists, Marxist and otherwise, argued that the state was the great evil and should 'wither away' in favour of a classless and autocratic society where 'the administration of things would replace the government of persons and the streams of life would flow more abundantly'. Normally, however, the takeover of the state machine by purportedly revolutionary governments has led to a brisk and energetic upthrust of central interference. It is arguable that the Soviet Union is the most solidly centralised state in human history. The same is true of the corporate states of so-called fascist persuasion, nations like France building on the imperious effectiveness of Napoleonic-type practice, and the highly centralised nations of the developing third world.

Geographical dictates, historical traditions and other factors effect the flavour and quality of each nation-state, and this argument is not a moral one: it is not suggested that one administrative methodology is preferable to another. For instance, France is probably less decentralised, in a local government sense, and the United States much more decentralised, in terms of states rights, than the familiar bipartite local-central administrations of the United Kingdom. By and large, however, the nation-state with the cash economy has usually meant a steady movement towards a society characterised by massive public management, increasingly of a centralised nature.

This is particularly meaningful for the treatment of social issues, which, more and more, have fallen within the orbit of central government. Although, in Britain, one associates welfare politics with the radical political wings, it is salutary to recall that old age pensions and industrial insurance were first introduced into Europe by the Bismarckian government of nineteenth-century Germany. Right across Western society the story has been the same: public health, the relief of poverty or support of social casualties, the organisation of the police and legal machinery, and the education system have all, practically everywhere, become the major province of the central state. When one turns to the actual day-by-day management of social provision, as opposed to its diverse political or philosophic beatification, the ubiquitous nature of the centralist state becomes ever more apparent.

To take the United Kingdom as an instance once more, the 'nationalisation' of social provision is very much a fact of life. Local agencies deliver the goods, as it were, on a local government basis, but they are largely subservient to the parent ministries and departments of Whitehall. The planning decisions, the exchequer control, the statutory obligations, the insistence on standardised approaches: they combine to offer the citizen a national and heavily centralised frame of reference. A century ago a small municipal borough would have enjoyed, through its Watch Committee, its own little police force; it would probably have a School Board to organise the education of its children; it might conceivably have had a local Board of Health; it would have played a leading part in one of the Poor Law unions. There were the inspectoral and other control of the central bodies, but these were frequently frail and rarely overwhelming. Now the Home Office, the Department of Education and Science and the Ministry for Social Services are very much in the box-seat, and, with recent local government reorganisation, the size and uniformity of the agencies has increased. We have a National Health Service, an intricate and comprehensive public health code, a national system of welfare for all forms of social casualty, tantamount to a national education service and tantamount to a national police service. Assuredly these collectivist tendencies have brought splendid benefits in their wake. The point at issue is the focus of their supervision, which has become, undeniably, more and more a centralised focus.

It is, nonetheless, the spectre of Prussianic old age pensions that should haunt the liberal mind. They remind us of the universal application of social expediency. They remind us that all nation-states, capitalist or communist, require a centrally-supervised legal and police system, a centrally-overseen education system, a centrally-based welfare system and a centrally-controlled public health system. And they are required, not just because it seems a beautiful thought or a morally respectable one (indeed, sometimes to avoid such beauty and respectability of thought!) but because they are essential for the everyday sustenance of the society in question. It is very near the old leftish saw, about bourgeois sops thrown to the proletariat to appease revolutionary impulses, except that the left are about the same game as the right. It may be that, as a society becomes more and more urbanised and industrialised, the administrative momentum towards public centrality grows unstoppable.

It is not easy to separate the one from the other, as the spiral of a more elaborate economy entwines with that of a more complicated bureaucracy. Today's army of public servants, equipped with their specialised and sophisticated weaponry of officialdom, are an extremely far cry from the Tudor monarch with his hardworking but small secretariat, utilising the mutual reliance of the Tudor squirearchy for the maintenance of good order. That classic amateur, the Tudor magistrate, levied rates and dispensed justice, and generally helped hold the commonwealth in one piece. It is vital to recognise that they lived and ruled over a nation-state and a money economy, and that the fundamentals of our national community remain unchanged. What has drastically altered has been the internal workings —economic and social, and thus political and administrative—of that national community.

This might be seen, in part, as the 'rationalisation', of which Max Weber wrote so acutely. As society develops more complex forms, so does it tend to evolve more rational, more formal and more standardised practices. The highly specialised civil service, for instance, rather than the sixteenth-century JPs; a solid, even inflexible, organisation across the nation, for instance, rather than sporadic and haphazard local effort. One aspect of this is the proclivity towards the large-scale, be it state or private. Ours is a world of vast commercial corporations, huge general hospitals, elaborate trading emporia, nationalised industries and multinational companies. Ours is a world of the ICI, Shell, the National Coal Board, the Thompson Press, Granada and the Prudential. Just as the nineteenth-century school was linked with the nineteenth-century factory, there is possibly a similar comparison between the corporate giants of the economy and the establishment of the large comprehensive school or mammoth university campus.

We must also face the possibility that the onset of an all but total centralism is partially the consequence of what Oliver MacDonagh and others have identified as the inexorable tendency of modern administration to procreate. This is the inner component of administrative momentum—the sheer urge of bureaucracy to reproduce in its own image. 'Large ants', it will be recollected, 'have small ants upon their backs to bite 'em, and small ants have smaller ants, and so *ad infinitum.*' Scientists threaten us with 'clones', the exact genetic replicas of existing human beings; administrators have long since learned the secret of such disturbing reproduction, and the phenomenon of what the medievals would have called 'much-governed' countries shows no distinction in terms of political philosophy. To east and west of the Iron Curtain, national management is a forbiddingly costly and labour-intensive industry. Whether we think it good or ill, few would argue that, in quantitative terms, the central bureaucracy was not large and powerful.

That, then, is the situation at present. Like most other ships of state, we are steering in the same direction, however varied in political hues the colours we nail to our masts. Much is the same. It is a nation-state based on a commercial economy, and, like all societies, its actions in so far as they regard social provision, are principally dictated by social expediency, by the natural desire to sustain and strengthen the existing economic and political ambit. As we shall consider in the next chapter, the theme remains constant of social ills being assessed relatively, by reference to the wants of (to employ an old-fashioned term) the ruling classes. That theme seems a permanent fixture of civilised society. It is the internal modifications—the industrialised slant on commerce and the parliamentary slant on nationstatehood—which demonstrate the change from four hundred years ago. And, with these projections, economic and political, has arisen the full-blooded drive towards centralism in social provision; the state has become more complex and centralised in all its doings, so has the character of and the response to social problems.

Chapter 4

The Reaction Against the Centralist Approach

Has the advent of an overpowering centralisation of the British administrative machine rid the country of social ills? It was earlier
argued that, thus far, all civilised societies had suffered social ills, so
much so that it was possible to reverse the equation and suggest that
the existence of social ills was a yardstick of civilisation. Put another
way, there has been so far no 'equal' society. In each civilised grouping there has been a relativity, in terms of life-styles, which could be
designated as non-equal. Superior wealth, and its attributes, such as
housing, food, leisure pursuits and so on, is an obvious example, but
superior health, superior education and even superior obedience to
the law may also be traced. This is an organic assessment; it is
temporary and internal. It does not take an absolute norm for all time,
of poverty or ill-health; it examines the society as it stands at a particular time. The poorest in England now are richer than their
ancestors a hundred years ago and richer than their counterparts in
other parts of the world. It is worth clarifying that point, for many
people carry in their heads a kind of minimal concept of poverty or
crime or ill-health. It is a movable concept, applicable, in this sense,
to a given society at a given time.

Sometimes it is suggested that our own society is more equal than
it was, that incomes are less exorbitantly spaced in range, that we
stand equal before the law, that we have equal educational opportunities, and that, through the National Health Service and other
means, we have equitable chances of good health. My contention is
that this, at best, is using a different criterion of social troubles, and,
at worst, it is misinterpreting the situation by refusing to accept the
interplay of relativity. Granted, then, an uplift in the minimum
standards of health, income and education over the last century and a
half, the question still remains as to whether these have been fundamental or merely proportionate shifts in the social commonwealth.

It was previously hypothesised that all civilised societies play out
their relativist positions in a rough-and-ready Marxist way, with a

controlling group or class, who glean most benefits from the system, but who, to preserve that system, are prepared to release sufficient of the fruits of that system to the lower orders to keep everyone relatively —the adverb is not casually chosen—happy. One might argue that so-called 'revolution' occurs when that ruling faction or class, will not or cannot absorb the balm of social reform successfully, and the whole body politic is threatened with collapse.

Despite the many egalitarian and classless claims made upon its behalf, the United Kingdom is still largely in this position, in that, although the minimal standards have risen and some of the gaps have narrowed, the middle class retain their pre-eminent status. A consensus summary of the several divisions of the population according to the occupation or profession of the head of the family suggests that 30 per cent might be called middle class, and the remaining 70 per cent working class. (This reflects both the Registrar General's five-point occupational scale and Research Services Ltd's six-point socio-economic grades.) The major point of distinction is between the professional, managerial, supervisory, non-manual grades and the manual workers, skilled and unskilled. The contention will be that these 30 per cent—and the figures have remained pretty well untouched over this century—continue to uphold a highly favourable position.

There are overlaps. The poorly-paid teacher watches the highly-paid car worker; the young underpaid bank clerk notes his contemporary on big money in the building trade—and the myth spreads of declining middle-class incomes as opposed to the huge wages paid to the working class. But the total picture, especially when extended over career (for professional incomes tend to rise more steeply than manual ones) and especially when the application of income is considered (the comparative ease, for example, of the 'salaried' man obtaining a mortgage), remains like a rerun of the Forsyte Saga. Apart from promotion, 80 to 90 per cent of non-manual grades have an expectation of an annual salary increment, compared with 20 per cent of manual workers, and, whereas over 90 per cent of the former's income is basic and predictable, 25 per cent of the latter's pay is 'unpredictable', that is, it derives from overtime and payment by results. Despite the popular view that incomes between the professional and manual classes have closed over the years, the average money income for the former was seven times greater in 1960 than in 1913; the average rise for the latter was only eight times, hardly a significant closing of the gap.

In point of fact the chasm between high and low incomes remains critically wide. Let us get to the raw meat of income, beyond the confusions of taxation, and search out post-tax take-home pay. In 1973 some 18 million taxpayers took home between £625 and £2,500, that is from £12 to £50, and, of course, there was also the residue of non-taxpayers, the very poor, pensioners and so on, below that minimum figure. Three and a half million took home anything from £2,500 to £12,500, that is from £50 to £240 a week, and this included 150,000 between £6,250 and £12,500, that is £120 to £240 a week. It excluded a fortunate 2,000 with a post-tax income of more than £240 each week. Seen against a norm, at that date, of about £31 as the average manual worker's weekly wage, and the point is underlined. It is instructive to note that, between 1961 and 1971, the basic wage rates for manual workers increased by 78 per cent, while average salaries rose, over the same period, by 92 per cent. Although, of course, overlaps exist, the 70 per cent of the population who may be designated working class were solidly entrenched among that 80 per cent of the tax-payers who had less than £50 each week. They carried, no doubt, some of the luckless middle class with them, such as those clergymen and teachers whose increments had not kept pace with the average for their class.

If one turns to actual wealth and the sheer holdings of capital, property and resources, the gap is more dramatically apparent. In 1973 20 per cent of the population owned 84 per cent of the nation's wealth, leaving a mere 16 per cent to the other 80 per cent of the population. Indeed, 1 per cent of the population owned something approaching a third of the country's wealth, and the chances of achieving such wealth are augmented by family connections—two-thirds of those who died in 1956 with assets of £100,000 or more were fathered by men who left estates well over £25,000. Again, that 20 per cent figure is deliberately chosen as being the nearest approach to the 30 per cent figure used to embrace the middle classes. A half of that 20 per cent were worth between £15,000 and £300,000, but it is the other half who are as interesting. After all, we are fairly well acclimatised to the ornately rich. The other half (that is, 10 per cent of our population) control a fifth of our country's wealth, at an average of £10,000 each. Now £10,000 is none too much: it would usually be composed of about £6,000 worth of house, £1,500 worth of household goods, the same insurance, and £1,000 or so in savings.

Just as one could emphasise the spectacular wealth of those 30,000 or more lucky people with over £30,000 of holdings, one could as easily silhouette in stark outline the extremely poor. Each week 8 million national insurance payments were made to old age pensioners, widows, the unemployed and those absent from work because of sickness or injury. As many as one in four or Britain's households were dependent on national insurance benefits as a prime section of their income, and that apart from almost 3 million means-tested supplementary allowances. A. B. Atkinson estimated that something a little under 5 million people were living below the national standard assessed by the Government. Peter Townsend has drawn attention to the 13 million people covered, directly or indirectly, by the five dependency groups (retirement pensioners, long-term out-of-work, the disabled, fatherless families, and families with four or more children). One must seriously consider the proposition that there are many in full-time employ whose families fall below the poverty line. In 1970 (when the average manual wage was £28 per week) over a million men earned less than £17 before tax, of whom 300,000 received less than £14. In the same year two-fifths of female workers earned less than £13, and a fourth of them less than £9. It has been calculated that what are coolly referred to as families living in 'wage-earning' poverty number 220,000; that is over a million people, including, most alarming of all, 600,000 children.

Thus one speaks not solely of the millionaire and the pauper. One speaks of a gradient of wealth and income. It has ever been fallacious to assume concern for the bottom drawer of acute poverty, presuming that everyone above is fine and dandy. One must preserve the image of the slope from poorest to richest, with a rough-and-ready point, a blurred phase, where the balance alters from unfavourable to favourable. One must compare, therefore, not just the opulence of the landowning aristocrat or industrial magnate with the fatherless family of six cabined in some dreadful slum. One must also compare the ten or so millions associated with wealth of £10,000 or more with the ten and more millions possibly associated with life slightly above or just below the poverty line.

Of course the government outlay on social security is itself a fable of riches, almost all of it directed, characteristically enough, from the centre. About a tenth of the gross national product—some £4,000 million, the largest item of the government budget, the equivalent of education and the national health service combined— is expended on social security benefits, almost as if an effort was essayed to mirror the public charity of ancient Rome. But poverty is not a static nor an absolute concept. To be poor is 'to be placed in a particular relationship of inferiority to the wider society'. It is contended that for over two-thirds of our population this inferiority is, in slowly mounting degrees, the fact of life. Money (along with parallel aspects like the form in which it comes, salary or wage; how long it takes to earn, leaving what sort of scope for other activities) remains a significant key to life-styles.

It determines, for instance, the crucial question of residence, so much so that, arguably, the nation is moving away from mixed housing stock towards what might be termed the 'Wimpey-corpy' syndrome. In other words, those whose professions earn them monthly salaries repay mortgages on owner-occupied premises, and those whose jobs earn them weekly wages pay rents for council houses or flats. This might, of course, conceivably be an improvement, in that the major holdings in slum areas are often still privately rented properties.

A brief survey I recently conducted in Liverpool revealed the following pattern of comparison between a 'model' surburban and a 'model' lower-working-class block of an average hundred houses:

	Suburban Houses	Inner-ring Houses
	%	%
More than 1–5 inhabitants per room	4	12
Share accommodation	1	42
Normal amenities (hot water, bath, toilet)	90	19
Owner occupied	50	15
Privately rented	8	60
Council properties and miscellaneous	42	25
Working-class proportion	43	94
Middle-class proportion	57	6

Thus the housing stock tells against the lower-paid, whose accommodation is frequently substandard. The North-West Regional Study of some years ago, showed that several working-class enclaves had fearful overcrowding—Kirkby, for instance, had almost a fifth of its 50,000 population living in overcrowded dwellings. In the Tyneside conurbation, in 1966, there were 17 per cent of the population living in six or more person households with more than one and a half persons per room, while, turning to lack of amenities, out of every hundred Tyneside households, fourteen had no hot-water tap, twenty-three had an outside WC but no inside one, nearly four had to share even an outside WC and nineteen had no fixed bath. Needless to say, the Tyneside conurbation is largely working class.

One could take a whole series of examples, demonstrating how social class and income determine life-styles. Turning to two of the four major social ills reviewed in previous chapters, the same remains true. There is little need to harp on the heavier incidence of crime in working-class districts, despite the occasional colour of an urbane graduate master-criminal of the Raffles variety. In 1967-8 the six most socially deprived wards in Liverpool showed the severest stress in terms of crime, as of a series of allied social maladies like debt, children in care and possession orders. Taking the heavily proletarian city of Salford (only 11 per cent in social classes I and II) the Principal Medical Officer reported that, in 1966, Salford children were among the lightest and shortest, most prone to respiratory disease and most highly infested in the country, and that the incidence of handicapped children was sorrowfully large. He also pointed out that one in four households had no proper hot water supply, two in four had no exclusive use of a water closet, and one in three had no fixed bath. Equally revealing is the fact that Middlesborough, with the highest child population in the country and a huge working-class population, has a set of one of the longest GP lists in the United Kingdom. Two-fifths of its doctors had over 3,000 patients, compared, say, with Harrogate or Bournemouth where the lists are less than 2,300. In *The Lancet* of 15 June 1974, Professor Townsend propounded the fearful calculation that 40,000 deaths from Social Class V between 1959 and 1963 could have been avoided had National Health treatment been equitably available. The manner in which the middle class have benefited in health *vis-à-vis* the working class is explicable not only in terms of private medicine and private insurance schemes, but in the way they have exploited services better and found, in their residential areas, better services on offer.

It would be possible to take other aspects of social life—job opportunities, transport, libraries, leisure facilities—and make the same case. Of principal concern here is the effect this has on educational attainment, and, in turn, the kind of education service offered, and whether this, too, is substandard to begin with. The National Children's Bureau's *Born to Fail* following the same agency's telling volume *From Birth to Seven*, highlighted the interconnection in dramatic style. Speaking of its massive cohort of eleven-year-olds studied from birth, it pointed out that one in four came from a large or one-parent family, one in seven from a low income group (that is, 2 million out of the UK's 14 million children of school age) and one in four was living in substandard housing. As many as one in sixteen fell into all *three* categories, two per classroom, as the report has it. From this base, the document recorded its woeful account of the likelihood for these ones in sixteen of poor chances at birth (teenage mothers, weighing less at birth etc.); the likelihood of sharing a bed, with consequences of disturbed sleep and infection; the likelihood of unfavourable family circumstances, such as family ill-health or disregard of education; the likelihood of ill-health and physical backwardness (height, vision, accidents, sickness and so on); and a whole series of other unpleasant 'likelihoods'. They all add up to one in four being, by eleven, 'maladjusted', three times the normal average for ordinary children; one in six requiring, at the same age, 'special help', nearly three times the ordinary norm, with, on average, this disadvantaged 'one in sixteen' group having fallen three and a half years behind the norm in reading scores by eleven.

Few need now (one hopes) to be reminded of the educational handicaps wrought by social disadvantage, especially at its blackest depth in educational priority areas. Like the millionaire-pauper twinning, one is well acquainted with the Etonian-inner city school early school leaver pairing. A figure often used—by the Plowden Report and the DES for example—is that 10 per cent of schools contain a large majority of deprived children, and the *Born to Fail* records would bear this out. The danger is that some interpret this as meaning that the other 90 per cent have some form of even chance of educational progress. As with poverty (or health, or law and order) one must talk about the 'poorest', that is, the *most* deprived, rather than the 'deprived' as an absolute total. Again, one must evoke the image of the gradient, with most at proportionate levels of disadvantage, until the crucial point when the high ground is attained.

As we saw in the introduction, the whole pattern of life-styles is interconnected. Housing, income, social class, health, social order and so forth all intertwine in a downward spiral. Or an upward spiral. There is a 'cycle of affluence' as well as a 'cycle of deprivation'. Given knowledge of a child's birth—its locale and its family—one can predict fairly reliably, for the majority of children, the outcome of their life—their health, schooling, jobs, marriage partners, housing, leisure —and thus, eventually, their children. This gives a hereditary element to our education system, which is truly amazing. When the Robbins Report logged 17 per cent of boys from 'non-manual' homes entering university as against 2.6 per cent of boys from 'manual' homes, it was narrating some of this fact. The children of the well-educated become well educated, and the children of the ill-educated become ill educated. This is, perhaps, put too starkly, but such social mobility as we enjoy is mainly concerned with the inner echelons of clerks and skilled workers. 'There is', wrote John Raynor, 'imperfect mobility at the top of the social pyramid, with two-thirds of the men in the higher occupational groups having had fathers in those groups, and with probably three-fifths of the higher civil service and higher industrial management emanating from social class I. Even at the same level of intelligence (itself strongly influenced by class patterns) the chance of higher education is twice as good for the middle-class child as for the working-class child.'

Reverting to our approximation of a 70/30 population split on social-class lines, one can project the following sequence:

	Start School	Reading Average and those at 7+	Success in Eleven-Plus[a]	5 O-Levels	Sixth Form	Higher Education
Working Class	70	47	8	6	4	1 or 2
Middle Class	30	26	18	14	8	4 or 5

[a] or, if cynicism be forgiven, the top stream of the comprehensive school.

All in all, the principle enunciated earlier of a haves/have-nots partition operating in social provision, almost as a talisman of civilisation, holds good, despite much-vaunted promises of equality of opportunity. For herein lies the slight difference: many educationists, teachers and politicians have grafted and struggled for equality of opportunity, and genuinely believed that the system had been transformed. Oddly, this is a view also formed by the middle classes on the defensive. The anti-comprehensive lobby and the Dark Riders of the Black Papers tend to argue that egalitarian policies have resulted in falling standards. They should not shout before they are hurt. It is akin to arguing that Christianity has failed, without any society having really attempted it. We have not had equality. Whatever may be our discontents, that is not the cause. Those of us who were naive enough to press for positive discrimination were innocents abroad: we should first have aimed at equality.

This is as true for input as for output. It is well known that provision varies critically from authority to authority, according to their resources, in turn dependent chiefly on social class and allied income. Howard Glennerster has calculated that increased expenditure on education in the 1960s was, in effect, allocated to the middle class in terms of a 112 per cent increase and to the working class as only a 76 per cent increase. He estimates that social class I obtains seventeen times the benefit of university expenditure as social class V, but pays only five times the revenue. So much even for an effort to reduce inequality. It is not too much of an exaggeration to conclude that things are, in fact, what they used to be; that social mobility has never been completely absent and that the social mobility of our age is not basically different from the social mobility to which Thomas Becket or Cardinal Wolsey might bear testimony. Some have claimed, perhaps a trifle colourfully, that some type of conspiratorial theory exists, whereby occasional blood transfusions from the proletariat are imbibed by the bourgeoisie.

Why have purportedly egalitarian practices failed so abysmally? The simple answer lies in a constant theme of this book, namely the interlock of social issues, which, in this case, meant that educational equality without social, economic and cultural equality was a non-starter. But it stemmed possibly from another cause as well. This celebrated interlock is, by that selfsame token, its own educational ambit, and, as the education system was highly similar across the board, the chance of its complementing the social context at any given point was a mere gambler's throw. Educational opportunity knocks; but it only knocks once. It knocks once for each child, but with a regular beat for every child.

Put another way, it is uniformity, not equality, of opportunity, and the two have become hopelessly confused. It is as true of other universal panaceas, such as the National Health Service, that there is a tendency for those who are already well situated to utilise their standing for favourable benefit. This is an arc in the 'cycle of affluence', for the articulate, assured middle class are able to negotiate the intricacies of such universal remedies more efficiently. An education service, as an act of social provision, offered free to everyone, immediately entails that to him who hath shall it be given. An education service, offered *in vacuo,* offers a more helpful chance to those not impeded by other social ills.

This raises the question of whether the central authority, acting through its local adjutants, the local education authorities, can meet the real needs of equal opportunity. It looks very much as if the sovereign state can provide the mechanics of opportunity, but not the chemistry. It is able, technically and legally, to proffer the same opportunity to every child. Every infant has an Oxbridge mortarboard in his satchel. All Souls awaits each five-year-old, just as, theoretically, the cardinal's palace awaited each medieval peasant. But the process is no more purely 'educational' for the youngster than it was pristinely theological for the serf. Moreover, the sovereign state appears to be concerned entirely with alpha at the expense of omega; the beginning, that is, and not the end. It is able, technically and legally, to set the game of equality in motion, but appears unable to guarantee equality at the end of the game. It fires the starting-pistol, but does not hold the finishing tape, or, even if it does, it has no control over the runners once begun.

Some would submit that this is how it should be. The liberal view would be that this is as much as the individual can expect; freedom to take whatever advantage he may of his public educational chance. A far leftist opinion might be that little more can be expected of a capitalist society, which always intended that the middle orders should continue to dominate, and that education was no more than a gentling of the masses. This, however, does little credit to the genuine pioneers who were convinced of the efficacy of a mechanical operation of educational opportunities, and who could, at least, point to the marginal dents made in the edifice of middle-class predominance. Nor does it take into account the wish, so frequently expressed, of the need for an intensely educated citizenry to realise the country's economic potential. The argument about waste of latent ability remains, in many minds, a strong one.

Equality must eventually, nonetheless, be concerned with consequence as well as inception. It must be about ends as well as beginnings; about children coming more equally to the finishing-line as well as beginning equally at the starting-gate. This is, unashamedly, a moral precept, based on that principle of social justice which allows each person a free choice of his life-style and role in society. Self-evidently, without the skill and knowledge, which education can crucially assist in providing, that informed choice is not possible. More of this anon; suffice it for the moment that this was, and remains, the credo of much educational reform.

There is other, admittedly impressionistic, evidence for doubting the ability of the central state to create such equality, even to move towards it in the mild and liberal manner of the 1930s and 40s. First, to repeat, centralism is not, of itself, 'socialistic', and there has been a constant delusion that state control or nationalisation is co-terminous with socialism. The theme of the analysis so far has been to recollect that the centripetal forces of administration have arisen because of and in conformation with socio-economic dictates, that these forces are active wherever demographic, urban and industrial conditions interlink, and that, in any event, central control is not, *vide* the Roman Empire or the French State of the sixteenth century, a novel phonomenon.

This is not to argue that radical opinion has not inspired, even occasioned, collectivist legislation; only that it has never become over-pitched in the direction of social equality; and, more significantly, it has often been couched, humanely and properly, in terms of social efficiency. It is commonly believed, for instance, that the post-war Labour Government had to nationalise the railways and the coal mines in order to salve them from collapse and retain them in the interests of all-round social efficiency. Many no longer quibble with other utilities being under public, often central control—planning, motorway-building, postal communications, water, energy, refuse collection, to pick briefly and randomly from the motley of possible instances. Taking the railways, however, as a test-case, their continuance and overall planning for public welfare rather than private profit or, as in this case, non-profit and decline, is not the same as offering consumer equality. As a doctoral student, I had free and immediate access to any number of libraries and archives, from the Public Record Office to the more obscure town halls of Lancashire. Probably the finest collection of documents and books in the world was, across the nation, at my behest, an Aladdin's Cave of historical treasures spread throughout the country. It often struck me as odd that the only inhibition on utilising this fabulous and gratuitous service was whether I could afford to get there! Public (for that matter, private) transport is not free, and, therefore, it is not equal. Like education, it affords the opportunity, so long as one is able to take it up. Perhaps it is an administrative accident that libraries are free and trains are not, or, more sceptically, it may be that libraries are a minority, even an elitist, service, whereas, trains might, if 'equal', be overwhelmed.

Further, one could claim that the nationalisation, not only of industry, but of social provision has not brought great advances in democratic control. Miners, let alone coal-users, do not manage mines, any more than train-drivers and porters, let alone passengers, run trains. The users of the health, legal, welfare and education services do not have much control either. There are local education committees and there are boards of managers or governors for schools, but their powers are limited by central statute. Dame Kathleen Ollerenshaw has estimated that, given the statutory requirements on education at state level, only *one* per cent of the budget remains for leeway and for local alteration. The House of Commons has, of course, a final word in all this, and one is not suggesting that participatory government does not, at its own level, operate with fairness and competence. Indeed, some would claim that its strong lead is the source of what success such services as education have so far enjoyed. The point is that, by the time the margins of control have been slowly eroded by everyone else, the scope for popular, local decision-making is tiny. In the actual school arena, the parents, teachers and children have precious little room for man-oeuvre.

As well as the confusion of centralisation with radicalism or socialism, there is, secondly, some impression that the state can do no more. Its maw is replete. If one inspects the pendulum swings of social legislative activity over the last hundred years in Britain, the following sequence presents itself. The radical Gladstonian legislation and the Disraeli-inspired social reforms of the early 1870s gave way to an era of relative legislative quiescence until the liberal reforms, associated with Lloyd-George, and the quickening of legislative activity in the war years of 1914-18. This, in turn, was followed by relative quietude on the social reform front, until, once more, the Second World War, and the so-called 'silent revolution' of the first Attlee administration, 1945–50. Another period of reforming somno-lence occurred, until the phase of Labour control of 1964 to 1970. Of course, these are waves or emphases, and not blacks and whites; it is a relative judgement, simply, that there was less socially orientated collectivism in the between-times, and, to be just, rather more man-agerial consolidation. But the expectations of the late sixties were dashed. However pleasing some found the libertarian reforms of that period (on divorce, capital punishment, abortion, homosexuality and so on), few would claim that there was a major extension of central interference, for good or ill, in social provision. The Land Commission or the Prices and Incomes Board look decidedly puny and wan when measured against such giant citadels of centralised social reform as the Public Health Act of 1875, the National Insurance Act of 1912, or the creation of the National Health Service in 1948.

We must consider, then, the possibility that the state can do no more. Hard as it tries, it has had its fill, and any more central control leads to administrative indigestion or worse. There are many, of all political shades, ready to testify to the waste and inefficiencies of overmuch bureaucracy. This is said not unkindly. The state has done a lot, and many of us would be in a parlous material plight, if it had not. The suggestion is not that it has necessarily failed, but that we cannot expect too much, perhaps we cannot even expect more, of it.

A third pointer towards the state's incapacity to create a more equal social context is the grassroots movement at local level. This localised and activist response is, admittedly, not new, nor is it as widespread as it is spectacular. Nonetheless, the outcrop of community groups of many kinds is an important phenomenon, in that it appears to form a converse response to seeking public good through state action.

Tenants' associations, consumer groups, community and neighbour-hood councils, parents' associations, student action, shopfloor and other types of worker engagement— there are dozens of examples of this process. Sometimes they formulate around a single issue, such as an airport site or a motorway route; sometimes they are thematic, such as consumerism or housing associations; sometimes they are work-orientated, from farmers to hospital workers; sometimes they are based, like a school's parents' association, on a generalised social role. By protest and demonstration, as well as by more conventional forms of committee and allied activity, they attempt to make a point or bring about a change. They are extra-parliamentary, in so far as they attempt to achieve their aims by direct, often local, forms of positive activity.

Some of them are extra-parliamentary enough to risk breaches of the law, either by demonstration tactics verging on the unlawful (invading rugby pitches; blocking thoroughfares) or refusing to carry out statutory requirements (rent and rate strikes, some forms of trade union activity). In this more extreme form, one recognises a dissatisfaction with the channels existing to communicate grievances at central level. The so-called Fair Rents Act and the Industrial Relations Act, operational in the early seventies, led sometimes to almost institutionalised opposition, in that councils and union branches seemed prepared not to accept the dictate of a central and sovereign parliament. A resurgence of national feeling in Scotland and Wales, an awakening of similar feeling in some regions, as well as an aspect of the problem of much-troubled Northern Ireland are akin to this. They represent a suspicion that the super-state cannot validly meet the needs of some of its component parts. Nor, of course, is this a merely British proclivity.

A key-word is participation. It is about people, in their various roles, having some say in the control or development of that role. Hence the parent-manager (or teacher- or pupil-manager or governor) of schools; hence the students' essays in obtaining more influence on the life and style of university and college; hence an unusual sequence of work-ins at a number of places of employment; hence the neighbourhood council and community centre; hence the community newspaper; hence the playgroup . . . The list, if not endless, is lengthy. In many walks of life and work, people seem readier or more pressed towards involvement, and that involvement is normally action-based. It is increasingly an action constructively for, as well as a protestation critically against.

In fairness to the state, it must be reiterated that this phenomenon is due to the state's success. To some extent, many of these local or communal activities are possible because central government has, over the last hundred years, created a solid base of material stability. Central government, and its local government agencies and partners, have laid on water and refuse and sewage removal, public health systems at many levels, an educational service, environmental coverage of all kinds, a formidable battery of parks, cemeteries, street lighting and all the other attributes and ventures of local councils, adding up to a massive national undertaking. However unequal, at this moment in time, our society remains, few would doubt that the levels of education, health, prosperity and even, in spite of some alarums and excursions in the cities, many degrees of law and order have risen. It has been argued by trade unionists and others that the working classes take out of the gross national product the same proportion they took in the 1880s; it is not argued that the gross national product has remained the same. Indeed, a well-worn middle-class argument is that it is they who procure this syndrome of the rising parallels of standards, with the working class always at a respectful distance behind. The gap, it is sometimes argued, spurs on the upper line to greater endeavours, and, because the chasm neither closes nor widens, the lower echelon benefits. So there is, at last, a heightened material corpus to distribute and (the two are in evident interface) an increased bureaucracy to enable some of the distribution to be on all brands of public activity from grid-cleaning carts to universities.

Many of the non-state or extra-governmental efforts at participatory or popular action are, then, made possible because the scope is available for them. A hundred years ago, as it were, men and women were struggling to attain that which we now, via the state, take for granted. Just the sheer struggle for everyday existence was acuter; after all, the tapped water supply and sanitation system we nearly all, with turn or twist of wrist, happily assume, is not much more than a hundred years old. But it is a further testimony to the state's fulfilment: having done all this and laid its stable foundation, the modern equivalent of struggles and protests are couched in different vein. It is the old historian's saw about change, coming where things are going well, rather than badly; the need for an inch so that people can aspire for a mile. Thus it could well be that a growing interest in community involvement is both a swing of the pendulum, away from perhaps the excessive centrifrugal interference of the last century, and also some form of forward motion.

It is important to analyse the evolution of these populist tendencies in order to place them correctly in their historical perspective. They are not, in practice, autarchic, either in the *laissez-faire* sense of the old style Victorian school, nor in the Utopian Socialist mood of Owen, Fourier or Saint-Simon. They are largely attempts by the public, grouped by locality or function, to win increased influence with the public realm. The time appears ripe for such open and direct management of affairs, but the limitations must be recognised in order for a proper and effective assessment of such a proclivity.

The first limitation is that the overall frame of reference has not changed, and, seemingly, is unchanging. We live in an omnicompetent state, founded on a cash economy. The second limitation follows from that, namely, that the fount of sovereignty lies irretrievably at the centre. The third limitation is also a consequence of the first, in that a nation-state, with a money economy (indeed, any civilised society to date) appears, with a somewhat depressing inevitability, to shape a political arena in which a sliding scale of disequality is maintained at the optimal point whereby the surety of that arena may be maintained. In simplistic terms, the haves will outvie the have-nots apropos wealth, health, law and order and education, as well as several other spheres emanating from these four major concerns. By their control, overt and covert, of the economy, the media, the political machine and so forth, they command the situation accordingly. It is not necessarily a vicious phenomenon, to be delineated in class-war terminology. Much of it happens spontaneously, automatically, even accidentally, and a considerable amount of folk-lore subscribes to the situation. For instance, it is not easy to persuade people, including teachers and including unskilled workers, that 'equality of educational opportunity' does not, in fact, work.

Thus the possibility that social issues, such as education, could be resolved by community or popular redress, must be seen as a modification within an existing framework, rather, than a complete overhaul of the framework. The realistic possibility is that community development might act as a monitor or as a check on the centralised state and that it might procure a more successful format for equality of treatment and opportunity; in other words, it might give more people more chances of better health, prosperity, schooling and so on.

Two moral imperatives are coupled in this regard. One is the belief that a more equal society would be a step towards social justice for all; the other is the belief that people should engage more freely and fully in decision-making processes. There is, as we have seen, some ground-swell of feeling in support of this joint ethic. Many people genuinely believe in some degree of equality, even if only at the level of 'opportunity' and of fair treatment in, for example, the hospital service. Many people also believe in the right to be heard in the processes of management that affect them. But, throughout civilised history, the creed has seldom been sufficient. For modifications within the commonwealth to occur, the acknowledgement and consent of the well-to-do or ruling faction has been, more or less, indispensable. There is, of course, stout support for such progressive policies among middle-class ranks, but it would be dewy-eyed to expect a major stand-down of the professional and managerial classes on enthusiasm for a cause alone. The question remaining is whether, or to what extent, these groups are worried and saddened by the symptoms of urban decay, violence and collapse. Here the community educator and his thoughts meet those of the demographic specialists, the military experts, the prophets of worldwide doom, the conservationists and the broad panoply of urban investigators. Across the West the warnings of urban degeneration are sounded, and the degree to which they are heard by the middle classes may well be the key to the degree of community development permitted in our society. It is argued that Britain would never suffer the slings and arrows which have assaulted American urban life, but, of course, there is another side to that medallion. Ours is a tight, little series of conurbations, without the huge hinterlands of the USA wherein the badgered American middle orders can retire. Like cholera in the 1840s, urban decline could affect, and is in fact affecting, the suburbs adversely, and, in this kind of *extremis*, it has been usual for the middle classes to give ground.

I trust this sounds not too sceptical a viewpoint. It seems to me the most human and natural explanation. Few of us would welcome complete breakdown and chaos of a type which benefits few, and, least of all, children. The case for community action and control is a formidable one. On the one hand, it represents a vehicle which might improve the quality of opportunity and participation and equity in our society, at a time when the state machinery seems unable, of itself, to help much more. On the other hand, it represents a medium which might possibly temper some of the alarming prospects of future existence in the grey, anonymous conurbation. Viewed and propelled carefully within its historical context, rather than with energetic blindness, as an ideal *in vacuo,* it proffers the beginnings of a social policy in which both moral opinion and social expediency could be combined.

And nowhere more so than in education. Before, however, devoting space entirely to a possible construction of a community-styled education system, there is an important problem, very much concerned with education, that must be faced. It concerns the way in which the larger entity, the state, might relate to the smaller units of community identification; as a projection of this, the way in which those frontmen for the central bureaucracy, the professionals, relate to their clientele at community level. It is next proposed to examine this issue of the overall pattern of community development.

Chapter 5

The Pattern of Social Provision and The Community

By far the gravest administrative problem facing any moves towards localised participation is one that has haunted British, even Western, society for many decades. It can be put simply. The kind of material well-being, domestic comfort and technological apparatus most of us enjoy, and indeed expect, can only be operated on a large scale. The natural focus for immediate influence on our day-to-day lives is, conversely, on a small scale. For example, few would deny that water supply and the treatment of sewage can be most efficiently provided by widescale, even national, organisation. It is to do not only with the capital finance involved in expensive undertakings but with the necessity of planning and balancing resources in the general interest. Alternatively, the referential frame of everyday life is much smaller. The Redcliffe-Maud Commission, which led to the reorganisation of local government in 1974, commissioned, although hardly utilised, a piece of research which demonstrated that most citizens conceived of only a few streets as the ambit of their civic and social identity.

At the political level, this is where the contest exists between representative government and popular government. Delegates, normally elected on party lines for lengthy periods, are able, nationally and locally, to offer a public forum for debate, to make decisions about all manner of policy, and to lay down programmes of action. This is very much in tune with the large-scale nature of our complex national society. Simply, it would not be easy to have a referendum about each item of defence and foreign policy or about every decision concerning a nationalised industry. The notion is that, as it were, the population surrender their democratic rights to their chosen representatives, and that democracy is maintained by proxy. Unluckily, this scarcely operates at the local and individual level, where people sometimes find it difficult to cope with the remoteness of public decision-making. It has, for instance, been estimated that (in spite of quite widely believed myths about sponging) as much as a third of welfare benefits are not taken up, and one chief reason for this might be the intricacies and entanglements consequent upon having to operate national formulae.

This also illustrates the difficulties of the other side. Attempts, for example, to map out a national policy for educational priority areas founder on the variable incidence and typology of urban deprivation. There are rarely flat, uniform characteristics about any urban social issue, and a central government never finds it simple to mete out a just provision or solution for all degrees of the same problem. There is a strong case for administrative forms which can evaluate and solve problems at localised points.

The actual place of local government in this large-scale small-scale clash is an ambiguous one. Posed as the age-old question of the state versus the individual, does the intermediary agency of the municipality act as the co-belligerent of the former or the defender of the latter. Certainly, in the nineteenth century, the 'shopocrats' in the thriving northern towns saw incorporation as a bulwark against an inquisitive and over-interfering state, and there are plenty of instances of central-local feuds, of which several squabbles over comprehensive schools form but one example. Conversely, many individuals see the distant and unfriendly 'them' as an amalgam of town hall and Whitehall. The central and local protagonists of bureaucracy often fade imperceptibly into an official togetherness, and many would be hard put to distinguish whether the authority which confronted them was central or local in character. The recent rationalisation of local government may have contributed to this sense of distance and obscurity, for the units are, whatever their increase in mechanical efficiency, larger and more artificial in composition.

The single-purpose authorities of the Victorian era had by pre-war time slowly given way to the multipurpose authorities of today. To pursue the four categories of social provision used throughout this analysis, the old Local Board of Health, Burial Boards and Sanitary Authorities became part of the appropriate municipality in the local government reforms of the 1880s; the police authorities had, since the Constabulary Acts of 1839 and 1856, been a local government department; the School Boards were replaced by the local education authorities under the 1902 Education Act; and the function of the old Poor Law Unions was adapted by county and borough councils in the late 1920s. As the various sectors drew together, the strength of the relevant central body grew, so that, in this era, there is a close and critical connection between, say, the Home Office and the local police authority or the Department of Education and Science and the local education authority. Less noticeable is a detailed contact between the varied divisions on the ground. The multipurpose authority has not yet solved the poser of interdisciplinary concern. Hemmed in by the statutory and other forms of centralised control, each department does its thing for its own area, most of which are now extremely large in terms of popular identification. Where divisions of territory are attempted, they are frequently lacking in constancy, so that the children's section of the Social Services Department might use a pattern of devolution which is wholly different, say, from the catchment areas for primary and secondary schools created by their education confrères. The relative failure of social services departments, with responsibility for day nurseries and playgroups, and education departments, with responsibility for nursery schools and classes, to combine in the promotion of co-ordinated programmes of pre-school provision is a sorrowful illustration of the point.

To some extent, local government's very ambiguity is an apt summation. It is too small to combat the will of the central autocracy; it is too large to offer its citizens a day-by-day role in governance. It has neither the single-minded concern and energy of the old-style mono-purpose agencies, such as the School Board; nor the co-operative attack of the carefully interwoven broad-scale authority. The probable logic is to accept the trend of local government towards a growing subservience to centrality and, particularly in its rational, sizeable 1974 image, to recognise the local government departments as the field-officers, albeit still with representative oversight, of the nation-state's agencies. This would leave the way that much clearer for the systematic development of a much more intensified and low-profile scheme of local community control and assessment.

The tendency towards popular management is scarcely assisted by the fact that most people are not solely attached to one community. Indeed it would be truer to speak of 'associations' or 'communities' rather than of 'community' as an absolute. Especially in urban locations, many of us share differing communities: we live in one, work in another, find leisure in a third, and so forth. This is one of the reasons why, for instance, educationists are beginning to talk of the 'educative community', that totality of experience of which each person's or group of persons' education is composed. The parent of a schoolchild would be concerned with this, perhaps even anxious himself to pursue some further education, but it is likely that he works or watches his football in association with another grouping of his fellows. Coterminous economic, political, social and cultural communities are less rare than they were, as the cosmopolitan nature of expanding urban life militates against them. If anything, the very

complex mesh of role-location and function argues for a corresponding web of low-key participatory form, so that people can make their
point and influence felt, despite the confusing nature of social and
economic existence.

Where, nonetheless, interdisciplinary community approaches are
possible, they should be welcomed. The need for a global approach is
a compelling one, for the interlock of all community elements is now
inescapable. The idea that educational provision may be undertaken
without due regard for and as part of other forms of social provision
should now be laughed out of court. The local authority, like the
state, because perhaps it is so much part of the state, has found it
difficult to provide according to variable strengths and weaknesses
within its boundaries, as opposed to offering uniform treatments. The
concept of positive discrimination, of topping up the resources of
some as opposed to other schools, has not been a very practical proposition in certain areas. Animosities and vested interests vie with
inadequacy of evaluation to foil the best-laid plans, and, even when
disadvantaged districts are roughly identified, across-the-board responses are the rule. To use the pre-school example again, there has
been little street-by-street survey to assess the incidence of need and
prescribe the particular mix required. The Halsey Report on educational priority areas firmly recommended the idea of 'local diagnosis',
but, without some devolution of executive management to meaningful
local levels, this remains a troublesome proposal to implement.

The decentralised, cross-disciplinary community management team
emerges as a possible resolution. But it must be a firm and workable
approach, and not any kind of return to parish-pump politics and
toothless parish councils. Perhaps we should avoid altogether the age-
long dichotomy of central and local or large scale and small scale. This
could happen in two ways. First, the aphorism that he who pays the
piper picks the tune has frequently been used to defend excessive state
action. It is misleadingly based on the image of the state coffers
doling out funds and thereby laying down regulations about their expenditure. If anything, it is the state that is the piper—and the
individual in rates and taxes, pays and should, in turn, pick the tune.
It need not follow that the state machine should command as well as
provide. It is possible to view the central bureaucracy as a provider,
and the local community as the decider. The state, and its local
government agents, could hold the resources, the services, the wherewithal and the expertise as a sort of mart at which communities
shopped. The state would be like Hardy's 'President of the Im-

mortals': it would 'do all and know nothing'. Perhaps a series of national institutions—an Education Corporation, a Transport Corporation, and so on—would be available to contribute the necessary help and materials for locally commissioned remits. One prerequisite might be a 'nationalisation' of public finance. The anomalies of rating could be abolished in favour of a single, centralised taxation system, and then the Finance Corporation or Treasury could allocate, on a per capita or other sound basis, funds to each community, so that they could choose and purchase as might be deemed appropriate.

Of course there would be some matters which require national standardisation and safeguards. The state would have as now to establish a skeletal structure or minimal frames of reference in subjects like road-building or education, within which communities could arrange their own priorities and activities. This leads to the second way in which the central-local contact might be eschewed. Instead of the seesaw metaphor of that central-local duality, one might envisage concentric circles of community involvement. A 'smaller' community might oversee and house some playgroups, a school, a branch library and a group surgery, whereas a 'larger' community (composed of several of the 'smaller' variety) might oversee and house a college, a reference library, a hospital and a fire brigade. While still retaining the state structure, it would be not unlike Kropotkin's 'league of leagues' and 'association of associations'.

The concentric circles of community management would permit of a smaller, more fluent and more democratic process, and would steadfastly blur the sharp distinction of centralism and localism as it now exists. Ideally, economic organisation could play a crucial role by adopting similar formulae. For instance, market gardening might fall within the province of the 'smaller' and motor car manufacture within that of the 'larger' community; while some industries (aircraft production is conceivably one) would remain within the purview of central government. If a congruence of the social and economic aspects of community life could again be introduced, the pattern would indeed be a strong one.

Some services are, of course, managed on a regional or interauthority basis already, but the up-and-down see-saw metaphor still remains a safe image. It is a spasmodic and awkward format. The individual has little continuous line of influence, to say nothing of access, through expanding tiers in any particular service. In health, for instance, the avenue of doctor-clinic-hospital is obvious enough, but it is difficult to ascertain what the points of control are. Few could name the management board that supposedly runs their general hospital. Who runs what and, as meaningful, what powers are they allowed? These are the important questions. The appointment of watchdog committees (like school managers or some consumer protection) is a well-intentioned habit of representative government, and it is a formula for keeping a finger on the political pulse and giving an opportunity to channel complaints and suggestions. However, representative government, at national or local level, rarely permits too much of its executive power to slip away. It is not popular control in any thoroughgoing fashion. The extending tiers in education follow, roughly speaking, primary school—secondary school—tertiary education (further or higher). The parent, say, with a child at each stage, may find himself needful of negotiating with two or three sets of governors or managers, an education office and maybe a college or university body. The professionals, teachers or officers, can, like general practitioners, pass children and parents onward, ever upwards, and direct them to the points of egress into other elements in the system. It is not, however, an even, fluent routeway. It is jerky, to say the least. Furthermore, although parents and children are allowed access, they have comparatively little say in control, except in a triennial vote for a man who must somehow represent them *vis-à-vis* cemeteries as well as classrooms.

The success or otherwise of all forms of social provision depends very much on these professionals who either cater for the client or, as we have noted, know where next to steer him. Each citizen plays a series of passive roles. *Some* play *one* dominant one. In the community there are a set of professional 'social providers'—teacher, social workers and officers of all kinds, doctors and health workers, policemen and solicitors, all operating to combat the macabre quartet of ignorance, poverty, ill-health and crime. They play a dominant role in the relationship with their clientele of pupils, paupers, patients and prisoners. There are also others who play a similar kind of predominating part, such as the housing officer, the transport manager, the librarian, even the shopkeeper and the newspaper editor. Needless to say, each of these is or should be an expert, trained and/or experienced in that vocation, giving it his or her full-time career commitment.

What, in practice, this means is a highly specialised series of role-play, to which the citizenry relate in passive and reticent mood. So reticent, in fact, is this general mood that those who occasionally react violently are often felt to be an embarrassment if not a nuisance. One thinks of the angry father bursting into the school, the know-all patient endlessly visiting his doctor to parade his own self-prognosis, the so-called social casualty who outwits the social security officer, or, for the law suitably houses the classic of the genre, the barrack-room lawyer. No one, simply, enjoys being told how to do his job. A situation in which the specialists and professionals hold the clientele in however benevolent a thrall fits neatly with representative government. If democracy is, as it were, suspended for the duration between elections, the salaried officers can maintain the public services in the meanwhile, safe in the knowledge that public or electoral accountability is only periodic. This is not to argue that public opinion's weight or the activities of elected delegates (councillors or members of parliament) are negligible, merely that, as the officers are not subjected to much day-by-day popular control, it behoves them to sustain their expertise as skilfully as possible. Put negatively, the citizenry does not need to understand the mystiques of the various professionals if it has no primary power to influence them.

When one envisages a much more involved participatory process of community management, this dichotomy of professional and client is almost as troublesome an inhibition as the dichotomy of large-scale service and small-scale identity. Consultative administration founders on ignorance, and the professional cornering of specialised knowledge about public functions tends to preserve such ignorance. It appears to be a natural professional instinct to protect the mystique of one's calling, doubtless with a view to avoid dilution. This is a valid kind of anxiety, and the point should be met.

But it is too much to expect a more active client response along that sequence of professional-lay relationships, unless the clientele are better informed. With representative government, the issues are high, wide and handsome. For example, one might, at local or national level, vote in favour of candidates who are for or against comprehensive education. It is reasonable to anticipate that many voters would be able to grasp the broad pros and cons of such an issue. It would, nonetheless, test the same people's knowledge and thus judgment of the organisation of the local comprehensive school, and yet this is the mundane application of that same national policy which most nearly affects the voter and his family.

Education is an especially relevant illustration, for it is general education in all types of social provision which is lacking. The situation has become serious, even dangerous, as the tendency towards consultation grows. Each time an effort at democratisation collapses, be it in street, workplace or wherever, there are many ready to cry that 'they' are not ready for responsibility and that 'they' cannot be trusted with power. Setting aside the self-evident truth, that without experience of responsibility the requisite skills cannot be sharpened, it must be admitted that, when the blame for each such democratic collapse is apportioned, education must shoulder a fraction. Over the last few years lip-service has been paid in some fields to consultation. The planner may have knocked on the doors or halted the passer-by with his questionnaire. What sort of home, what sort of environment, what sort of neighbourhood would you like? These may have been his questions. He may have been dissatisfied with or dismissive of the answers; to be fair, he may genuinely have acknowledged them and included them in his appraisal, only, perhaps, to find them wanting and, in turn, blame his respondents for their shortcomings.

The plain fact is that few of us have been educated to answer that kind of question. What comprehension we have of planning or housing or education or health tends to be at a generalised level. Having been brought up on a diet of the War of the Spanish Succession, the square on the hypotenuse, the tin mines of Bolivia and the poems of John Masefield, it is not surprising that only a minority can grapple with the realities of dialogue with the professionals.

A further instance of the difficulty may be found in the recent election of parent managers and governors for schools in many authorities. This has been a liberal and genuine attempt to improve participation. There is already, however, some evidence that resultant changes are negligible, that the parent manager is often drafted from an almost non-existent electorate, that he or she, once nominated, finds the rigmarole of committee procedure either scaring or boring, and very little briefing or training has been offered the appointee. This is a grave matter. This has been a well-meant reform badly bungled, because a fresh angle on participation had to be bent to accommodate with the outmoded formula of management. The cultural and political realities were not sufficiently examined before embarking on this unthinking and shallow exercise. If it fails or, as bad, if it neutralises the parental voice in education, it will be a sorrowful day. The same could apply to worker-participation in business and industry.

One hopes this does not sound patronising, and it in no way suggests that ordinary common sense is absent from the normal citizenry or not of use in such cases. It is the criticism often levelled at that long established branch of civic participation, jury service, whereby, suddenly thrust into the majestic and awesome panoply of the law and faced with myriad points cast in a daunting jargon, twelve of one's peers can be bewildered and bemused, and sometimes end following the professional in blinkered style. It is the form rather than the substance of democracy, unless, by uncovering the magic of the professional conjurors, we make it otherwise.

I never realised how extremely inhibiting the teacher-parent relation could be until, removed from the educational contest where I had advocated and campaigned for increased home-school dialogue, I travelled, hastily and breathlessly, to visit a dangerously sick near-relative in a Manchester hospital. I joined the inevitable huddled knot of grey humanity, clutching flowers and energising bottles, who patiently await the commencement of visiting at every ward door in the kingdom. A minute or so before the golden hour, a houseman made his round. The ward was closed to visitors, and this even applied to my own relation who was critically ill enough to be lodged in a side-ward within the main ward. The houseman moved from bed to bed, not, as far as one could note, doing anything terribly exciting and, even had he wished to embark on some profound piece of medicine, each bed was equipped with screening curtains. So there was no necessity to shut us all out, thereby increasing, however slightly, the psychological stress on both visitor and visited. As he emerged, leaving only fifteen minutes of visiting remaining, I was about to upbraid this non-apologetic medico on the subject of his public relations, professional judgement and so on, when all the irrationalities beset me which I had pooh-poohed in parents when they spoke of their fears about talking to teachers. That somehow my poorly kith and kin would be victimised was the least of my instant worries which allowed this (in my view) incompetent to walk away unchallenged. It could, of course, have been a solicitor or an inland revenue inspector in a similar situation.

Perhaps this autobiographical extract may be forgiven if it can be deployed to illustrate a general point. Arguably, the professional-lay rapport is frequently under strain. The laity are worried because they are unprepared in terms of knowledge for the dialogue. The professionals are worried because they fear loss of status, and they retreat behind clichés like 'a little knowledge is a dangerous thing', as if their own knowledge, by some standards, were not 'little'. And if this quality of relationship were placed in a populist context, the stress would be well-nigh intolerable.

Here, however, the argument turns not just on the need for democratisation or equality for its own ethical sake, it also meets the point about the interconnectedness of social ills and social provision. If education or medicine or crime could be lassoed and branded like a mid-west steer, then a professional, an expert lariat and branding-iron master would be fine. But a lone ranger has limited value in the fields of social provision. Children are not educated solely at school, any more than all sickness is prevented or treated by doctors and hospitals. There is an educative dimension and a health dimension and a law and order dimension. We all contribute to each all the time. One cannot educate or medicate in a vacuum. The school attempting to go alone educationally is two steps removed from reality. The school is part only of the vast ongoing process, and that process is itself interlocked with the housing process, the incomes process, the welfare process, and so forth.

In that knowledge, then, of how education (or health or law and order . . .) proceeds, it should become part of the professional function to understand, relate with and guide the dimension with which he is concerned. If the expert wishes to enjoy an improved fluency and success in his task, then he must help the clientele to support him. To take a simple example, if the teacher is teaching reading by 'look and say' methods and the parent in a natural and proper desire to help the child, is using phonics at home, it could be harmful and is certainly wasteful. If the professionals can transmit some of their mystiques to the laity, the laity would be able to share the endeavour and the discussion with a greater sense of confidence and knowledge. If the dominant-passive character of the relationship could be adapted, first through dialogue and then through joint activity, the whole level of the quality of social provision might rise, because the entire effort and resources of the education dimension (or the health dimension or the law and order dimension . . .) would be co-ordinated and directed to common ends.

There is a telling piece of evidence to support this thesis. At the turn of the century health authorities and the public were in some despair over the debilitated condition of the country's physical well-being, and items like the results of medical examination of Boer War volunteers were highly disheartening. It was during this era that the medical professions, by no means the least conservative of the callings, began to off-load a substantial amount of their stock-in-trade to the public. Through general practitioners, various forms of advertising and chemists, but chiefly through health visitors and clinics, they 'de-professionalised' themselves by allowing the citizenry, and especially the mothers of young children, access to a store of medical information. The whole kit and caboodle of saws and hints about pregnancy, babyfoods, vitamins, nappies, solids, weight, clothes, orange juice, early training, and a host of other items especially about early child development, were all transferred to the nation's motherhood. They were transferred with such gusto that, within generations, much of this has entered into our national folk-lore and is handed down, granny to mother, by word of mouth or demonstration. This has happened to such an extent that when one compares an understanding of how to mix, measure and mete out babyfoods with, say, the teaching of reading, one is told not to compare a 'natural' or everyday skill with a professional skill. The fact is that, in a successful attempt to raise health standards, the medical professions had to take the public into its confidence, school them in the basic elements of healthy living, and rely on them to build and maintain a bedrock of physical well-being.

The process of community development and community politics invites many specialists to do exactly the same, and indeed, invites, the medical people to do the same some more. It is no accident that the Halsey Report on educational priority areas helped coin the designation 'educational visitor', in the hope that the analogy with health visitors would be remarked. The proposition was that, like health, education rested, for better or worse, on a communal interlock, and that to safeguard and improve the intellectual, as opposed to the physical, well-being, of the public, similar tactics would need to be deployed. In 'deprofessionalising' himself, the specialist 'part-professionalises' the client, so that he can disport himself more adequately in the appropriate dimension. The important clinching point is that the client's engagement is unavoidable. Given the concept of an educative dimension, the parents cannot avoid some form of engagement—it might be woefully feeble, even crucially damaging; but the parent cannot opt out of 'educating' his child. Whatever he does or does not do has an effect. The objective of 'demythologising' the professional is to make that effect positive, helpful and at four square with what all agencies are doing for the upkeep or benefit of the clientele.

The example of the doctors also indicates that anxiety about status need not necessarily be valid. The doctors have not suffered, in salary or repute, because their potential patients can handle many minor ailments and because mothers are better informed about child-rearing. At best, the GP acts as health consultant for the health of the community around him, and, perhaps freed from many trivial aspects of physical welfare and able to concentrate on the major problems of his patient-list, his status is protected. Similarly with teachers, if the teacher were seen to be the consultant for the educative community, the specialist craftsman who convened the educational resources for his catchment community and monitored and directed accordingly, his prestige, hopefully, his salary, could be lifted. It is not a reduction in professional know-how, a wholesale bonanza in which the teacher's birthright is sold to all-comers so that, as teacher, he becomes redundant. It is rather a radical, lateral shift in the character of his professionalisation, whereby the teacher's stature itself would rise, as he came to be regarded, not as someone who taught children, but as someone who was the steward or overseer of the community's educational potential.

If there is to be popular involvement, there must be popular knowledge and assurance. Teachers still fear for interference with their work, but they must recognise that their best hope is to take the public into their confidence and allow them a supportive role. A colleague, recently preaching this doctrine, was sarcastically asked by a teacher whether, if he was the Captain of the *Queen Mary,* he would allow the passengers to steer the ship. He agreed that he would not, but argued he would tell the passengers where the *Queen Mary* was heading, and inform them if it were sinking.

Democracy is about *informed* choice. It has not been surprising that, where parents have been thrown in at the deep end of educational consultation, they have asked for extensive canings and thirty minute's spelling every day. It is not surprising that they object to vertical streaming, the opposite of their own school experience, if no one has bothered to confide in them. 'How', I was recently asked by a mother, 'can my four-year-old and my seven-year-old sit in one class and be taught by one teacher at the front?' How indeed. No teacher had had the time or the wit to explain carefully and, if need be, repeatedly to that mother what was happening to *her* child for five hours every day. This is not to suggest that all 'progressive' notions (no spelling tests, no corporal punishment, and family grouping) would be acceptable to parents once they did comprehend the pros and cons. These are controversial areas, even among teachers, but that only underlines the necessity of making the debate open, full and lucid. Valid options and selections can only be founded in knowledge. If there is to be popular oversight—and the trends seem to point in that direction for some aspects of our social life—then it must be based on informed choice. The demythology of the professions, including teaching, is the prerequisite for this.

A pattern of social provision, therefore, which tried to embrace a participatory or popular component at local community levels, would need, within the centralist state framework, to establish two elements. One would be a structure of 'concentric circles' of social provision, in order to acquaint the economies of scale and popular identification more smoothly; the other would be more fluent professional-client dialogue, in order to ensure that participatory influence is based on informed, not blinkered, choices. And now one can turn, emphatically and particularly, to an analysis of a possible education system for such a community in such a situation.

Chapter 6

The Educational Community

Those of us who have been concerned with 'community education'
have amassed a considerable amount of descriptive literature about
how the community school might operate. Both the theoretical implications and the present state of practical experimentation has had
fair coverage in book form and through the media. The application of
the principle to pre-school provision, notably in terms of a mother-
orientation, is now well rehearsed and, indeed, reasonably well
proven. The application of the principle to the primary school, chiefly
in terms of improved home-school relations and a sharper concentration on an environmentally-centred curriculum, is as well-covered.
The application of the principle to the secondary school, mainly in
terms of a more life-centred syllabus and a broader usage of the
school plant for the whole population, is generally well known now.
The application of the principle to further and adult education,
mainly in terms of a wider range of vocational training and talk of
recurrent education, is, if not so well discussed, at least part of the
great educational debate.

In each of these cases, there are a number of illustrations, dotted
about the country, but principally at a school-based, rather than an
authority-based level. Two allied elements are sorrowfully lacking.
The first is an all-through continuous illustration of educational provision for a community, whereby the two-or three-year old entering
the system, may see the way, evenly and fluidly, ahead through an
educational avenue, community-orientated. Put negatively, one hears
of mothers attached to pre-school playgroups who are frustrated by
seemingly closed-door policies when their children reach school-age;
one hears of primary children, used to a socially engaged educational
attack, baffled by the narrow and introverted academicism of their
secondary school; one hears of secondary school-leavers, the happy

not my marking.

novitiates of an excitingly relevant adolescent education, disappointed by the tawdry dryness and aridity of their further or higher educational experience. Or, of course, the reverse, with parents and children 'liberated' by a move upwards from a secluded nursery class, a dulling, over-formal primary school, a chilling and tedious secondary experience, to the relevance and stimulation of a splendid college course.

The second absentee is an authority structure in which community education happens laterally. This may be a little unkind. There are authorities which have bravely tried to instil both the precept and the practice of community schooling into their areas, attempting to devolve administrative power to local and school levels and to encourage heads and teachers to alter their educational style to suit community needs. Partly because of the autonomous nature of the schools system, it is difficult, even within these rare examples, to discover solid phalanxes of pre-schools or primary schools or secondary schools or further education agencies, each series of which link together in concerted pattern. For instance, one could scarcely find a normally-size district of about 15,000 or 20,000 souls, and, hand on heart, boast that its half dozen primary schools formed a coherent nexus of infant/junior community education.

Lines of latitude and longitude are what are missing. There is no horizontal (by geography and administration) nor vertical (by chronology and strata) network, in which, comfortably and confidently, community education is practised. There has, of course, been some gain from the autonomy allowed schools. It has at least permitted of the gallant and inventive pioneering in the community education field which has been continuing and increasing since before the Second World War. But so many of these institutions remain like beleaguered desert fortresses, with insufficient *Beaux Gestes* to go round to allow for massive extension. This outpost-like quality is reminiscent of the difficulties encountered, according to George Bernard Shaw and others, of practising Christianity in a non-Christian climate. As with Christianity, community education has a social or collective aspect. While obviously not as metaphysical or broad-sweeping as Christianity, it does require some togetherness for its implementation. Just as the Christian ideally needs neighbours to whom service and help might be proffered, the community school cannot, by definition, go it alone. One cannot undertake community development privately, any more than one can properly be a private Christian.

There is, incidentally, a further analogy. Many people regard themselves, unfairly and incorrectly, as practitioners of both. Thus, when one is propounding the virtues of either code, there are as many, of the same mould, character and background, ready to say 'we're already doing that' as 'this is completely impractical'. As with the social attitudes of the Christian ethic, there are sufficient instances of what Her Majesty's Inspectorate call 'good practice' to be quite confident about the outcome if the few became the many and eventually the all. What we lack is a systematic and full-blooded attempt to consolidate the gains of community education, an attempt not only implemented thoroughly, but one capable of sound theoretical validation, so that neither officials nor teachers can, like 'Sunday' Christians, fly under, if not actually false, then certainly dubious, colours.

In brief, how would—how could—a local education authority structure its organisation format to provide a thoroughgoing system of community education? It is not enough to draft a blueprint at some remote drawing-board. It is necessary to invent a new structure, or modify an old structure so that it actually works. It is the 'actuality' of the system which is important. Ideal and real meet in the actual. It is, on the one hand, scarcely enough to chase a vision, however beatific, of some idyllic educative Arcady, if it is plainly outside the reach of the resources and personnel available in the immediate future. It is, on the other hand, hardly sufficient to operate a highly efficient and methodical and cost-effective schooling machine, if it fails to approach the philosophic objectives of the exercise. Historical parallels abound, as do educational illustrations, of both visionary schemes and impeccable management producing abject failure and misery.

This is why substantial space has been allotted to a careful examination of the organic growth of the whole theme of social provision, so that fine-sounding notions might be tested against the temporal lessons of society. Certain ground-rules might be extrapolated, some of them doubtless truisms, but nonetheless worthy of recollection:

1. that education is a part of social provision, interlocked rigorously with other branches of social provision, and not existing as a purely academic entity *in* social *vacuo*.
2. that social provision, including education, is largely determined by the prevailing social and economic framework of society.
3. that, throughout civilised history, the degree of social provision has been geared to sustaining societies at the optional balance of stability with inequality, as between, roughly speaking, the haves and have-nots.

4. that in the era of commercialised nation-states, more especially in their urbanised, overpopulated, industrialised form, the public sector of control has not only grown (irrespective of purported differences of political and economic ideology) but has become increasingly centralised, and that this applies quite definitely to social provision, including education.
5. that there seems to be some need and some evidence of a mild swing of the pendulum towards a *devolution* (and the word is used advisedly; it is assuredly not an *abdication*) of that power, plus some testimony of a ground-swell of community-type activity to that end, much of it in the 'social provision' arena.
6. that this need can be entertained in terms both of an 'ideal' of social justice and a 'real' of social expediency, and that the prerequisites may well include *participatory* as opposed to *representative* influence and control, alongside a corresponding 'deprofessionalisation' of the specialists *vis-à-vis* the laity.

Two lessons stand out clearly from this summary with regard to education in the United Kingdom today. One is that the chances of a pure democracy and a pristine egalitarianism are (and as, morally and ideologically speaking, I am myself a convinced egalitarian, I conclude this with gloomy pessimism) negligible—but that the time is ripe and the occasion suitable for a major and rewarding advance in that joint direction of more democratisation and more equality apropos social provision. The cash nexus and the central power of the nation-state, with, culturally, politically and economically, the middle classes securely placed, does not appear to be in any fundamental danger. Strangely, its chief danger may be in not making that pleasing major advance, and the resultant collapse which might occur if it failed to permit it would bring little benefit to anyone, least of all the already most disadvantaged. The first lesson, then, is something about limiting objectives and not overreaching, not out of timidity either of belief or action, but because the overvaunting ambition might prove fatal.

The second lesson is in consequence of this. It requires some acceptance of the centrality of power together with its playing out of that power through the local authorities. It probably requires some acceptance of the basic idea of a money economy, whatever its constituency of public and private mix. It means, in brief, sticking with the system. It does not mean accepting the system root and branch. It means recognising its shams and deviousnesses, but keeping faith—critical and reformist faith—with the system. Some would say this is the distinction between the 'revisionist' and the 'revolutionary'. My argument would be that this is a fallacious distinction. If a distinction exists, it is between the 'actualist', who attains workable results within the organic social frame, and the pseudo-idealist who achieves nothing and risks much. If achievements were a criterion, the 're-visionist' should often carry the 'revolutionary' mantle.

There is a wing of the progressive social and political movement which, like the nineteenth-century Utopian Socialists before it, is anti-state and is anxious in their own phrase 'to fragment the system'. It has roots, too, in the *laissez-faire* purities of thinkers like William Godwin, in that it ascribes to the individual total rights in regard of the state. But, it is fair to comment, the state is the conglomeration of the individuals and groups of individuals that compose it. Like the poverty or health or criminality or education gradients, one cannot easily assess when the state starts and the individual finishes. The teacher, like other public professionals, is in a most ambiguous position. To what extent does he perpetrate the evil of the state machine, and to what extent is he, as puny individual, oppressed by that malevolent leviathan?

More practically, the public weal consists of massive physical and personal resources. One turns one's back upon them at some peril in the mundane sense of their day-by-day utility. In the educational field, the rejection of all the capital plant, experience of teachers, school meals services and the rest of the paraphenalia verges on the naive.

The educational twig, as it were, of the anti-state or anti-establishment branch of radical politics is, of course, the 'deschooling' or 'free-schooling' sector. Attempts to establish alternative educational agencies *outside* the public sector may be rewarding in experimental terms, although, as yet, there are few signs that any transferable models are emerging. They are, almost without exception, genuine, well-intentioned schemes; but they are unhistorical. The free schools, to their cost, fail to recognise the true, albeit regrettable social and economic process that determines social provision, in a society such as ours, including educational provision. In their historical interpretation at least, they are non-Marxist.

By deliberately opting out of the so-called system, they engender unnecessary opposition from other teachers and administrators who are suspicious of the once-off exotic bloom which seems incapable of being transplanted in native educational soils; they make themselves sadly vulnerable to failure because they are automatically without access to the existing educational resources and supports; and they run the risk of being branded as self-indulgent for their troubles, because they are seen as choosing the vivid spectacle rather than the hard graft of schooling. The free-schools are misleadingly titled, if not in method at least in management, for, technically, they are 'private' schools, outside the realm of public accountability. The free-schools are forgetful that, especially since the First World War, the changes that have occurred in British education have mainly emanated from inside (witness the pleasing change in the climate and approach of the English primary school) not outside. The counter-claim might be that these alterations are not 'fundamental' but so long as the counter-claimants insist on arbitrating on what is 'funda-mental', that remains a circular argument.

Above all, the free-schools, by and large, fail to grasp the idea of the state as a conglomerate of its members. This is not to defend the establishment, and much has been said already in this book which is highly critical of the system; it is to grapple with the possible, rather than to fulminate about the immoral. Granted all the inequalities and injustices, even the corruptions and conspiracies, the public education system is, technically and legally, the public's education system. It should be the task of the community educator, or whatever other type of educational reformer, to make actual and real that legal and technical truth.

In the baldest phrase, therefore, any plan for educational provision in an area should be seen as a modification, however disruptive in degree, of the present set-up. In the clearest possible statement, it should be about what a local education authority should do and be-come over, say, the next ten years. This plan attempts both to antici-pate and mould trends; that is, it tries to sense the broad journey education is likely to take and to promote discussion of the most productive routes that might be followed.

There are a welter of cues about national proclivities. In 1973 there was the Government White Paper, *Education: A Framework for Expansion*, on education over the next ten years, and its acceptance of the need to embark on longer-term policy-making over the next decade. That spawned the Circular on nursery education, which re-ferred, if a trifle obliquely, to several of the recommendations later to be made about the under-fives. The Halsey Report of 1972 (*Educa-tional Priorities*) was concerned with education priority areas, and it indicated a unified pattern of approach to urban education, par-ticularly in its community setting. There was the James Report, with its telling review of teacher-education, alongside its indications of the form higher education and professional in-service training might take. Then there was the Russell Report on adult education, which also drew attention to the peculiar requirements of adults in working-class environs. There have been reappraisals of examinations and a splendid buzz of activity in the curriculum development field especially in terms of more life-related syllabi. There has been, and it continues, a wholesale reorganisation of secondary education, with a baffling complexity of variations throughout the country, and, with middle schools beforehand and changes in further education—one thinks of the rise of the polytechnic—afterwards, the institutional side of education has undergone a number of alterations. There have been many strides forward in home-school relations, not least with new procedures for school management which have begun to include parental representation. In many ways the plans outlined here will embrace the pointers enshrined in these documents and developments.

As for the interlock of education and other forms of social provision, there have been several instances, within the education authorities themselves, of services being offered of a socially supportive nature. It is not a novel idea. Meals and medical services have been available for some time, but, more recently, there have been many extensions of individualised treatments, by way of counsellors, home-school liaison teachers, education visitors, remedial teams, social and psychological units and so on. The Home Office's Urban Aid Programme has also recognised the interdependence of elements in the social context, in an attempt to succour blighted urban districts with open-ended grants. In particular, Urban Programmes, numbers nine and eleven, took up many of the recommendations of the Halsey Report. They proposed all manner of educational devices, such as education visitors, toy libraries, play centres, teacher-social workers, although with a concentration on the pre-school effort. The Department of Health and Social Services has stated its determination to break what Sir Keith Joseph, when its secretary, christened 'the cycle of deprivation', and it put in hand preparation for assistance and training in parenthood. Several of the Home Office's community development projects, with their pilot interdisciplinary attacks on urban problems, have also included educational schemes, notably in Coventry. This acceptance of the interconnection of education along with other essays in social amelioration is an illustration of the main thesis presented here. To some extent, it has been reflected at local government level, with 'community development' and 'area team management' projects.

So the time is apposite for a long, systematic look at the system; and the occasion is ripe for an effort to rationalise and unify into a coherent whole these many strands. It means, of course, that few of the detailed proposals made in the remainder of this book will strike with the explosive force of bright originality; rather is this such an attempt to seek out a unification of the educational service.

First, however, there must be a goal. An education authority has a statutory obligation to provide certain schooling and other facilities, but it is surprising how easily one can become overfamiliar with the exercise, allow it to meander through the motions, taken for granted and with little basic appraisal. Space and compassion forbid a weighty investigation of all the possible definitions of goal, but some statement, however personal, is necessary. It is a statement which has already been foreshadowed by the previous analysis of social provision as part of the historical process. It is a statement which takes into account the determinants at work on social provision and the traditional, even the ineluctable, role of education, as well as the moral overtone without which an educational goal would be an empty and sterile thing. Predictably, it sees education as of social, rather more than as of academic, character, and as about adults as well as children.

The goal of the national education system and of its local counterparts, should be, in my view, to give each individual child and adult a full and continuing opportunity to realise his or her best self, both as an individual and as an active participant in the social, economic and cultural life of the community. This opportunity should, as far as is legally and technically appropriate, be open-ended. It should be an enabling rather than an inducting process. It should enable people to reach independent judgements about their future, rather than induce them to accept standpoints decided in the past. This is something of a departure in educational history, for education has been the medium for transmitting the heritage of a society to that society's novitiates, in order to prepare them for it and thereby preserve the status quo. A decision to unlock the close-endedness of an educational system, whilst unashamedly ethical in justification, is not entirely out of keeping with the historical setting of our era. As we have seen, ours is a society of pluralism, of tendencies towards participation and democratisation, of contention over what once were regarded as fundamental truths, even of permissiveness.

There are those who may mourn this, but ours is such a society. We may not be able—we may not, in the last analysis, be allowed—to shatter the basic structure of national unity and the cash nexus, but, within that structure, considerable margins are and could be permitted for multiple choice in a number of social and cultural fields. This being the case, the teacher refusing this role would be failing in his duty, both in a modernist sense of drawing out each child as fruitfully as possible and in the historic sense of preparing each child for the sort of society prevailing. Ours is to certain limits which are, one hopes, expanding limits, a society where citizens make choices. Education should enable them to make such selections honestly, positively and constructively. In that the school is and should be the microcosm of society, one cannot educate children for a democratic community in an autocratic agency and through autocratic media. One cannot equip the citizenry of the twenty-first century as if they were about to live in the nineteenth. It has been said that we educate children as if they were going to be our grandfathers. Because of the giant forces for conservation in the educational system there is an alarming time-lag between the condition society has reached and the stage at which the school has arrived. One of the driving-forces in the community education movement draws its strength from this historic gap between school and community. Few institutions, so the historical record would suggest, can long remain in functional order if they are out of sorts with their social setting, and community education is eager to gear the school more fluently to its communal context.

The imbalance of advantage and disadvantage is an important element in that prime characteristic of civilisation, inequality. A meaningful dimension of this imbalance is the area of choice. The degree of choice permitted each person is according to the relative complex of inhibitions facing all of us. There are genetic, physical, domestic, social, geographical, economic, cultural and a host of other inhibitions, or lack of them. One hopes that other agencies will be doing what they can to temper the inequality in these fields. What education can attempt is an assurance that the choices are *informed*. Educators should be less concerned about the choices in themselves as opposed to their quality and the expertise with which they are made.

The life-style of a person and a community, eventually of a region and a nation, should rest principally on the choices made by that person and community. Education should ensure the choices are as informed as possible, for democracy is about informed, not just any old, choices. The education system should be designed to give the citizenry the information and the skills so to practise. The teacher should sharpen the social competence of children and adults. He should not be so bothered about the standards and mores adopted by them, nor should he try overmuch to foist values on them. People should, within the frontiers allowed them, invent and construct their own destiny. Teachers should provide them with the tools.

A current illustration is in deprived areas, where many teachers are busily persuading children to master the falderals of O-levels so that a few might escape the miseries of slum-life. There should be no argument that, materially, this is no less than the truth for many—it has been calculated that two A-levels nets an average bonus of £20,000 over a working-life. Conversely, there are those who tramp the disadvantaged districts telling the folks not to be caught up in the dreary chase for paper certificates. Incidentally, the fact that some of these have any number of O-levels, a sprinkling of A-levels and a university degree leaves them open to some suspicion of pulling up the ladder. They have, nonetheless, a point to make. What is required is an education which presents the information, the pros and cons of a contest such as this, together with a development in each individual of the faculties to select wisely.

Education should be both the training-ground and the market-hall of choice. And it should recall that the children in the system are already members of a community and are already faced with issues about which they must decide. It is not a question just of preparing children abruptly to become conscious of decisions about consumerism or television or whatever when they leave school. They should, slowly, step by step, be eased, throughout their schooling, through a growing awareness of and capacity for such problem-solving. No one expects the five-year-old to make earth-shattering decisions, but it is more likely, that, as an adult, his decisions will be mature, if, according to his age and intellectual and emotional range, he is helped in an extending consciousness of the issues that do face him.

The major message of this pronouncement of goal is a rehearsal of the theme of the educative community. This means, on the one hand, that education is consistently affected by the social and economic context in which it takes place; but also, on the other hand, that education is a theme permeating the whole of this social and economic context. It all adds up to the need for a radical shift in the education system to keep abreast of these feelings and developments. The tremendous interest throughout Europe in the principle of 'recurrent education' encapsulates the mood and the concept. It rejects the 'apprenticeship-bound' model, which sees education as a once-off preparation ending for most in adolescence; and it also eschews the 'second chance' model, whereby a fortunate few gain another bite at the educative cherry as mature students. It emphatically proposes the 'life-long' model, with education seen, continuously and actively, at the behest of everyone. It is not seen, however, as a passive transaction, with knowledge acquired in banal, second-hand fashion. It is articulated in terms of active problem-solving, with children and adults constantly utilising educational resources and facilities to adapt to or, if they so wish, modify the rapidly changing vocational and cultural landscape.

Education must no longer be open to caricature as a few hours at school for children for a few years of their pre-adult life. It must be viewed as a total, life-long experience, with the home and neighbourhood playing important parts, and everyone contributing to and drawing on this educative dimension of the community. Indeed, one must be at pains to emphasise that this, whether we like it or not, is exactly how the process occurs. This is a conscious recognition of that truth, and an effort to face it creatively and positively. To use the analogy of health, yet again, education is not something one is 'doing' or 'has done', it is something one 'has', like health, in varying degrees of 'good' and 'bad'.

The overall and pressing need, therefore, is for the education system to enter into dialogue with, comes to terms with and direct this educative community, offering a service which remedies the weaknesses and reinforces the strengths of the areas it serves. It requires a pattern of community education agencies—schools, colleges, and the like—to take up these shifts of emphasis, negotiating and channelling them as productively as possible. There is, of course, considerable argument about the present nature and definition of 'community'. Without becoming embroiled in that convoluted debate, let it suffice that one speaks chiefly of the 'educative' community, that group or association of citizenry served by the educational agency in question, and, by that token, influencing it in turn. The 'educative community' of this kind has two main sets of parameters, necessarily interlocking.

1. There is the ambit of social and cultural interaction. This is precisely the social and cultural arena in which the school or college can exert its influence on the life and minds of the people. Conversely, that same arena—the neighbourhood, the home, the street, the peer-group—influences the school and the response of the pupils or students within it. In sum, it is the totality of experience of all those concerned in the educational process, their effects one upon the other.
2. There is the ambit of administration and control. This is the geographical and managerial statement of that same social and cultural mutuality. It is the territory served by the school or college, and the

ways in which its inhabitants are assured or assure themselves of watchful control on the plant and resources at their educational disposal. It is the administrative skeleton to give shape and form to the flesh and blood of the educative community in its social and cultural being.

The first, the socio-cultural ambit, demands an institutional response, that is a scheme of agencies which guides and monitors the educative community from birth until death for every individual. The second, the administrative ambit, requires, naturally, an administrative response, that is, a formal pattern of direction and control emanating from the educative community. The warp of the one and the weft of the other could constitute an educational mesh which, in establishing the educational network for an authority area, would perhaps make good the two basic inadequacies described at the beginning of the chapter, namely the absence of a systematic, vertical line of educational facilities and the absence of a systematic, horizontal stratum of educational administration.

It is intended to suggest a formula for creating such a network, dealing, first, with the *institutional framework*, and, second, with the *administration framework*. Although it is trusted that the formula is capable of general application to any authority, large or small, rich or poor, urban or rural, it has been decided, for ease of illustration, to cite a model. This does not mean that authorities of this type and size are being canvassed; it is purely a sample authority to show how the formula might be applied.

The chosen authority is a metropolitan district and, thus, an education authority in its own right. It is urban, industrial and intensely populated, with close on 300,000 inhabitants. Of these 53,000 are children, from the newly-born to school-leavers, split 15,000 nought to five years, and 38,000 five to sixteen.

There are 90 nursery classes, primary schools and 15 comprehensive schools. For simplicity's sake, separate infant and junior departments have been ignored and comprehensivisation has been jubilantly assured.

Now read on.

Chapter 7

The Institutional Framework:
COMMUNITY SCHOOLS AND COLLEGES

1. *Pre-school*

If it is agreed that education follows the path from just this side of the cradle to just this side of the grave, and if one conceives of a toddler stage before children are ready for school in any traditional sense, then a thorough consideration of pre-schooling is necessary.

One must also take account of the considerable volume of evidence alluding to the critical significance, intellectually, socially and emotionally, of the child's early years, nor should one forget the constant historical theme of education as a form of social provision for those with social deficits. Just as the sick cannot perform a complete and normal part in society, the ignorant, however defined, whether child or adult, cannot play a normative role either. 'Ignorant' is not used pejoratively: obviously, the three-year-old is automatically bound to be 'ignorant' in that sense of an adult society. There is another consideration, possibly more important, and that is of the three-year-old already viewed as a member of the community, not merely as one destined to join it in the future. Thus the little boy or girl enjoys similar rights to his elders, and might legitimately expect that his pre-schooling life is not only preparatory for later experience, but something to be relished of itself.

In attempting to plan pre-school provision, one finds an educational sector which illustrates perhaps more vividly than any other some of the principles already established; namely:

1. the younger the child, the heavier its reliance on the parent, especially the mother, and, conversely, the stronger the influence of the parent on the child. The continuous theme of the powerful influence of home and social placement is, therefore, most apparent at this stage, so much so that most efforts to educate the child without the active engagement of mother or other close relation could be wasteful. If the child is, for instance, secluded in a nursery class on half-time attendance, then those fifteen hours a week, pleasing

though they may be in themselves, could be rendered futile, if, for the rest of the time, the training and attention is of a variant nature.

2. the younger the child, the more closely enmeshed the interconnections with health, welfare and other agencies. The university student could at some points, sensibly distinguish between the purely academic and the purely medical or physical in his or her life-style—and even that is only relative to the under-five, where any such form of distinction is almost impossible and usually invalid. The need to see education as but one element of social activity alongside health and physical well-being and alongside income and other items which dictate the life-style of the home and thereby the child, is crucial.

3. the younger the child, the more intensely concentrated the ambit of his identification; or, at its simplest, when catering for young children, one needs to operate at the most local of local levels. Accommodation must be close at hand, and it must fit the peculiar needs—shift-times, length of journeys, workplaces—of the families in question. To take again the example of the half-time nursery class, nine o'clock until noon: it has little appeal for the mother who has to work an eight until two shift, or for the mother who, high in a block of flats, must perforce, accompanied by a couple of even smaller children, negotiate four arduous journeys for the privilege. The case for local diagnosis is at its most lucid with the under-fives. The needs, forced and natural, of the under-fives are highly variable, and, luckily, the children are often as adaptable as the necessities are wide-ranging.

What is required is that most mind-bending objective of administration—the programme that combines coherence with flexibility. We have had some flexibility, and much of it has been rewarding. But there is the nursery class located in the primary school because space is available ... and space is available because of depopulation, which means less demand for nursery places. And there is the nursery school built next door to the brand-new day nursery ... ostensibly a welcome liaison, but, in cruel factual terms, a duplication of valuable resources on two sets of toilets, dining equipment and so forth. And there is the playgroup energetically established by two or three enthusiastic women in street 'A' ... and, although one can scarcely cavil at such eagerness, it might have been more effectively located half-a-mile away in street 'F'.

We have had some coherence. This has usually been the dogma of the nursery class or school. The nursery class, operating a standard half-time or full-time educational programme, with perhaps only peripheral parental engagement, has undoubtedly several splendid advantages. It is probably suitable for a good many children. What is challenged is the doctrinaire view that for all children, and, as pertinent, for all mothers, this is the one and only answer. This is a wasteful, even a dangerous concept, and, when linked with the notion of nursery education on demand for those who desire it, it provides an illusory shadow, rather than the substance, of coherence.

The EPA Report, *Educational Priorities,* recommended the correlation of the advantages of the three diverse forms of pre-school treatment, namely the sound child development activity of the nursery class or school, the full-day welfare and health coverage of the day nursery, and the positive parental involvement of the best playgroups. To these might be added the home-visiting programmes, convincingly pioneered in the West Riding. Some areas (notably at Coventry with its Nursery Centre, with its day care and nursery accommodation, plus a coterie of playgroup annexes) are moving towards this goal, but the problem of obtaining liaison between the statutory departments—educational and social services—and then between the statutory department—oddly, social services rather than education—and the voluntary sector appear to be well-nigh insurmountable in other authorities.

However, the 'Halsey Hybrid', as the nursery centre plan is sometimes known, offers a valuable baseline for local exploration. It is apparent that, at a low level of territorial or population area, a coordinated programme of pre-school provision needs to be constructed according to the requirements of the given locality. My own proposal would be that, for reasons which will, hopefully, become apparent, the catchment area of the primary school might be an appropriate arena. It is, admittedly, tiny for a variegated approach, but the need to operate at an intensely small level must be paramount. Variety could be promoted by a close alliance of all the pre-school districts within an authority. For instance, if a shopping precinct or factory drew its customers or female hands from far afield, adjustments might be necessary, in regard of the provision offered in or near the shopping centre or workplace.

Given our average-sized urban authority of some 300,000 souls, with 15 secondary catchment areas, embracing an average of 6 primary feeders each, that is 90 *in toto,* a chain of command might be instigated of:

1 pre-school co-ordinator at authority level.
15 pre-school organisers at area level.
At least 90 pre-school assistants at local (i.e. primary) level.

The initial task would be carefully to sound out the needs of each locality, and also its strengths. Some home-visiting programmes (like the Van Leer pre-school project in Liverpool's Netherley Estate) uncover untapped personal resources in the community among mothers, for example, willing to help other mothers. It would be the job-remit of each pre-school organiser to help the community mobilise its own resources to meet its own needs, as well as to monitor the input of authority materials and personnel. It must be emphasised, too, that any interdisciplinary action, with the Social Services Department mainly, but also with services such as parks or libraries, would be doubly welcome.

The chief reason, apart from viable size, that one should plump for the primary catchment locale is that the primary school should be the cornerstone of the enterprise. The firm argument against this would attack the early institutionalising of youngsters and the inroads made into the public-spirited initiatives of the playgroup movement. There are four counter-arguments:

1. the admitted fear of the school as an 'institution' is a circular debate: the sooner mothers and toddlers can move in and change that climate of feeling, the sooner the fears will be disposed of.
2. it is an administrative convenience, and its use as a pre-school base was recommended by the Department of Education's Nursery Circular (21/73). It exists, and, in existing, is a fabric and a set of resources not quickly to be pooh-poohed. There is now some experience of the installation of nursery classes in primary schools, the dissemination of which could be valuable, and, if nothing else, it rids pre-schooling of its 'draughty church-hall' image. Also, many parents would already have older children in the school.
3. it provides for a welcome continuity in the child's more traditional schooling, for the transition to 'real' school could be smoother and less jerky.
4. it builds a logical and positive foundation for cradle-to-grave community education, for it inducts both child and mother to that ideal at an early and valid age.

The overriding consideration is that the primary school would be the hub rather than the location for these 'pre-reception units' (to label them thus for shorthand reference). The resident pre-school assistants would be centred there, but a whole series of possibilities might be entertained, which, hypothetically, might not require the presence of children actually in the school, and a series of possibilities which would be revised itself as the balance of need in the locality altered.

The following is a series of such possibilities, one or a set of which the pre-school assistants, working in close concert with her (or his, for that matter) neighbouring colleagues, might construct for the locality.

1. a traditional nursery class, albeit with mother-participation, probably running towards a blurred 'rising four' entry into the school proper.

2. a base for a mother-orientated playgroup or playgroups, which was also envisaged by the Government's Nursery Circular, and which, at this point in legislative time might fall under the aegis of the Social Services Department.

3. a unit offering day care over elongated hours, but offering an educational component. Naturally, one would hope for close association with the health and welfare services. One might envisage, over the years, the combined building or adaptation of pre-school, welfare coverage and clinic provision on or about every primary school site.

4. a hub for a home-visiting programme, whereby the pre-school assistants, and other staff, or eventually, trained and capable residents and mothers, would take on a mother-child visiting load of from one to two hours a week. There is some evidence that this, educationally, may be as successful a technique as any, and that an hour's weekly tuition, with the mother following up during the rest of the week, might have more impact than three or four hours a day collectively. In the interests of socialisation, at least one weekly get-together, on a playgroup pattern, could prove rewarding.

5. a base for mobile activity. The 'Playmobile' idea, pioneered in Liverpool, and now quite widespread, is of the bus converted for pre-school usage, which can, on the Mohammed and the Mountain principle, visit the clientele, halting in street or at block of flats for a pre-school session.

6. such mobility might be linked with the idea of this pre-reception unit being the headquarters of a series of annexes: other sites in the locality—the supermarket, the factory, even the 'draughty church hall' might be preferable spots, and, from the primary school HQ, the pre-school assistant would offer help and advice. She might offer ancillary services, such as cut-price stores, a toy-lending library and the very necessary training schemes for mothers and other participants. In the interests of scale, these might be more efficiently organised at authority or area level.

To add some verisimilitude, an authority of 300,000 population would have something like 15,000 under-fives, averaging 1,000 in each of the fifteen areas envisaged or something like 150 or so in each primary school catchment area.

There are other possibilities and criss-crosses of possibilities, but, overall, such a scheme would appear to approach the magical formula of coherence and flexibility. The one proviso—the one rigidity, perhaps—is the essential nature of a mother-orientation. It must now be widely accepted that pre-schooling *without* mother-co-operation is just not productive. Thus the pre-school organiser, in creating her pre-reception units, must seek out not only the complaints and demands of her clients but their positive assistance and suggestions. This would be the elementary stage of deprofessionalisation, in which the pre-school organiser would convene the active collaboration of as many mothers as possible in the education of the community's toddlers.

The working mother presents a problem, but some of the solutions suggested—home-visiting, varied hours, elongated days with welfare cover—begin to cater for these. The social contracts of joint maternal action in, for instance, the playgroup field, meet one of the major motivations for mothers working, namely loneliness, and the wish to find new social horizons. This aspect could be developed, with all kinds of clubbable activities for young mothers tacked on to the pre-reception unit.

It is here that the mother-centred toddler's unit joins the other end of the community educational circle. It is no more nor less than an exercise in adult education. It is the offer of an activity-based and realistic venture in life-long education, as mothers and, one hopes, fathers increase their awareness and know-how of early child development, of social and political organisation, and so forth. It is a pity that one cannot meet the other motive for the working mother—that is money—by paying mothers to engage themselves in a pre-reception unit. Especially in areas of underemployment, this could have social benefits. It would, for instance, be interesting to compare the social cost and efficiency of building a brand-new day nursery with the payment of grants or wages to participating mothers.

On any large scale, this is probably outside the pale of local government control, but, at least, a honeycomb of pre-reception units, coherent yet flexible, could give an enormous impetus to a full-run system of community education.

2. *School*

The pre-school could thus imperceptibly fade into the school proper, with the parents readily recruited for continued involvement and the children pleasingly inducted into the system. At four or five, full-time education would commence in the authority's network of community schools, and an immediate dilemma presents itself. In embarking on the provision made by an authority for, in this model case, its 300,000 inhabitants, one must also recognise two stout proclivities towards autonomy; in short, towards a situation in which the authority does not control. One is the technical factor, whereby, in law, head teachers and teachers preserve a considerable, if not always well-defined, degree of control. The other is the point constantly pressed that 'local diagnosis' is of the essence, that if education is inescapably a contributor to and product of a total environment, then its stratagems and devices must differ accordingly.

The problem can be set in more positive terms. How does an authority find the balance between allowing the necessary local autonomy and ensuring that what each school does is effective? It might be argued that, in many areas, this balance is cock-eyed if not reversed. Schools may make decisions about some general educational principles (streaming or non-streaming is an alarming example) but authorities make decisions about some internal practicalities (some financial aspects serve as an instance—day-by-day spending in certain authorities is rigidly watched).

If an authority wishes to construct a system of community education it must combine direction with freedom in clearly defined sections. It must lay down a lucid frame of reference, with whatever statutory force can be mustered from existing legislation, within which schools can then operate as freely and imaginatively as they choose. The question of who constitutes the 'authority' and the 'school' in regard of such decision-making is deferred until the next chapter on the administrative framework. It is the institutional framework which is presently under consideration.

A community school is a neighbourhood comprehensive school. It offers its services to its host community, in part because that community is already busily beavering away educating the children willy-nilly. Once the overall effect, good or ill, of the social context on education is accepted, any contrived grouping of children falls, as a concept, by default. If actual schooling is but a part of education, and if that education is subsumed largely into its social pale, then artificial removals of children could be heedlessly futile. The ultimate and draconian measure of such contrivance is, of course, boarding education, when the child is placed in lengthy, if temporary, exiles from his home and neighbourhood, and is schooled like an emigré in a foreign canton. Bussing and banding and other mechanisms for guaranteeing 'social mix' are steps in this direction. Simply, they exaggerate the potency of the school *per se*. The school cannot, in five or six hours, make good what is deemed to be faulty in the existing social order. The foundation for the effective and successful school is rapport with its host community.

One should not be inflexible on this. Reasons may arise which make state boarding or the transfer of individual children a humane and sensible act. Choice should not be completely obliterated. However, it is or should be the objective of the authority to ensure that the parents' natural wish for their children to attend the school within easy and convenient reach is not blocked by offputting or inefficient schools. Phrased positively, the authority should make certain that all schools are equally effective, so that the nearest one, the neighbourhood one, is obviously the best. The parent should no more have to search out a school of his liking than he would ponder over several ever more distant pillar-boxes before deciding in which to pop his letter.

The neighbourhood school should be a comprehensive school, and the adjective is used advisedly in the lower case. In the event most English schools are comprehensive, in that primary schools are comprehensive. The 'Comprehensive' row only begins at the arbitrary age of eleven. Once it is decided that all the children of the neighbourhood should foregather in their community's school, the question of selection also goes by default. The community school would no more select by whatever criteria had been invented by the selectors than the local baker would select his priority of customers by the colour of their hair. The commonality of the school's population is an intrinsic factor, and selection, at whatever childhood age, would be divisive. Primary schools exist 'comprehensively' with little or no difficulty; indeed, many would argue that the absence now for most of a selection hurdle has liberated and improved them.

Growing pains exist, but, with one or two exceptions which should not, of course, be overlooked, secondary comprehension has, even in traditional terms of examination performance, normally held its own where comparison is validly possible. The recent national increase in O- and A-level passes at a time when much of the country has been 'comprehensivised' is, at least, a sign that, in conventional terms, the situation is not worsening. As ever, one must recall the social context which plays a strong hand, irrespective of the school's institutional format.

But the community school as the educative focus for a locality's youngsters should be comprehensive in deeper senses. It should be co-educational, non-streamed and interdenominational. And that means a legal as well as an educational debate. An authority could probably construct a co-educational system, but the schools themselves might claim rights on streaming and, needless to say, the churches hold sway over denominational schools.

The educational point is that, once a community foundation has been agreed, sexual, internal academic and religious 'selectivity' is as disagreeable as the external academic 'selectivity' of the eleven-plus. There are signs that some in the clerical hierarchies have some sense of this; certainly the church-state division is not in the United Kingdom the contest it was, while, conversely, the character of the Ulster confrontation—in so far as it follows a schooling pattern—is scarcely attractive. The crux of the case might be religious teaching. An authority might approach its denominational confrères in a spirit of guaranteeing such doctrinal rights. In fact, a solution might be forth-coming of an all-round nature. Religious education is the only compulsory subject, and, in fair reverse, it is the only one teachers and pupils may refuse. It might be possible for an authority to prescribe a system of 'levying in' rather than 'levying out', for non-Christian parents (and with church attendances running at some 7 per cent of the population on a fine Sunday, these are probably numerous) often find pulling their children out of religious teaching an awkward and uncomfortable performance. If schools, perhaps, on an area basis, offered religious education of varying shades, say, first thing in the morning or last thing in the afternoon, then parents or pupils could 'levy in' be they Roman Catholics, Moslems or whatever.

Many church schools have a pleasing record in community education, and one should not forget that, organically, a community might be so predominantly Roman Catholic as to make its local school a Roman Catholic one in character. Similarly, one should not shy from the outcome of a dominantly non-indigenous population creating a school of a particular ethnic flavour. The argument remains constant. Education is the province of its social arena: the school must accept and work within that arena.

As for co-education, the most up-to-date research findings confirm the promptings of common sense, namely that, academically as well as socially, the co-educational school scores. In any case, for most of our children education is a co-educational exercise from three to—for college students—twenty-one or twenty-two, with the even co-sexual tenor of those fifteen or so years disturbed for some by a bizarre segregation from eleven to sixteen or eighteen. As for streaming, the critical factor revealed by most research surveys is teacher attitudes and skills. Indeed, many of our latterday problems in education—going comprehensive, going open-plan, going co-ed, going mixed ability—founder because we expect teachers reared in one dispensation to welcome its opposite and take to it overnight. It is an authority's duty, once decided on a programme of community education (or, for that matter, any educational policy) to educate its professional staffs to cope successfully with that programme. If mixed ability teaching is deemed by an authority to be, as it logically is, a facet of community schooling, then they should offer extensive in-service training in that field to its teaching force, as a *quid pro quo*.

Some would argue that this limits parental choice. A parent, it is pressed, should be able to pick for his child a single-sex, heavily streamed, denominational school. Apart from the sheer impracticality of parents mapping out the vast permutations needed to satisfy them all, why should sex, selection and religion be the significant themes? Why should parents have rights on segregationist issues and not on others, such as finance, times, curricula, holidays, staffing and so on?

Above all, we must emphasise the point that, at this stage, it is the child, rather than the parent, or, on balance, the child-plus-parent, who is the consumer. It is not the parent of him or herself. As such, the principle of non-segregation should, where humanly possible and practical, be maintained, as the locality's community of children meet in harmonious and non-divisive mutuality. This is an unashamedly social view of the school as the pre-adolescent layer or mini-format of the adult community. Whatever else, a divisive school system can hardly hasten the coming of an integrated social system.

It is an unrepentant and admittedly strong line which brooks little compromise. It places education on the level of justice rather than holidays—it does not matter so much that people can choose exactly how they spend their leisure; it would be socially disastrous if people could select, even buy, forms of law which suited them. In a way education is too important for individual whim: like the law, it has to be rigorously equal, regular and common.

Over against that somewhat uncompromising and vigorous frame of reference, one might turn to the heady liberties which a school might enjoy. The community-teachers, parents, children and any others concerned—could have much more freedom than is often now the case, for, by strict regulation, many features of school-life are steadfastly controlled. Money is the root cause of this. At its extremes, schools have a permit to do what they wish, as long as it affects expenditure either marginally or negligibly, even when their activities might involve weighty matters of educational philosophy. They have no permit, at the other pole, to act where expenditure is involved. These are overstatements, but they underline the chief factor in the process. The head teacher may have family grouping, an initial teaching alphabet reading approach, no music and so on. He might find it difficult to stop his school being painted and deploy the money on tape-recorders and other equipment this year. He might find it difficult to appoint an extra member of staff and manage without £2,000 of resources next year.

Some authorities are moving slowly towards local accountability, permitting greater scope for choice at the school base. It follows, from the principle of local diagnosis, that schools would differ considerably, not only because of the varying complex of strengths and weaknesses in any district, but also because the professional virtues and vices of that very pertinent factor, the teaching staffs, are served up in highly dissimilar mixes. The authority, having laid down the objectives for its educational system and having prescribed the organisational formula for the realisation of these objectives, should, as far as possible, hand over control to the school.

That means handing over control to the school community, including parents, children and others, and, as we shall discuss in the next chapter, that requires a particular brand of local management. It obliges an authority to place one hand on its heart and the other in its pocket, as it beatifies the ideal of democratic localism. It invites the authority to provide resources which are utilised according to locality-based or school-based decisions. This is the next stage down of the refinement of centralism proposed in Chapter 5. Just as the central state is, at that level, the provider and the authority the decider, so, at the lower level, does the authority reverse its role, and play provider to the locality's decider. With a series of checks and balances, first at centralist then at local authority level, to guarantee the interest of the generality as against the benefit of the locality, more and more decision-making could be rendered populist. It will be noted that the decision-making process is not exclusively initiated in the community. This proposal accepts the inexorable historical lesson of the over-lordship of the omnicompetent nation-state and seeks to modify and sophisticate it in order to achieve deeper and deeper levels of popular influence.

Although the authority would proffer its services as a helpmeet to its schools, the business of local diagnosis and prescription would effectually be accomplished by those whom it most concerned. The responsibility for judging what a particular school community required would be largely left to that community. If, to begin with, a district was lucky enough to warrant a new building, it would be constructed on the basis of localised discussion within such limitations as cost and safety factors, on what progressively-inclined American architects call the the 'charrette' principle. As any such new school would have a general communal role to fulfil, the local planning would be doubly necessary.

The quality and appointment of staff, administrative as well as educational, would be another feature. Some schools might decide that with voluntary help, they could manage without a cleaning or dining squad, and save a little money for school trips. Others might feel that teachers were more productive than materials, and improve the one at the expense of the other. The school, as a community entity, would play its part in choosing staff, a task already dealt with, to some degree, by school managing or governing boards.

Questions of times of opening and closure, of holiday dates, and especially of the extramural or 'use of plant' activities to be programmed: these, and other issues, could be locally settled. The whole substance of the school—its curriculum, its structural divisions, its timetabling, its choice of materials—would be, as now, at the behest of the school, albeit in the wider setting of the school community at large.

Naturally, the question of the school budget would devolve on to the school management body, as would the physical fabric of the building. Repairs, maintenance, decoration and all the other matters affecting the school would become a localised affair. Supplies and materials of all kinds would fall under the prerogative of the local school, and, in general, the day-by-day administration of the school would no longer be the direct responsibility of the authority.

The authority, in these regards, would be the servant rather than the master of the schools, supplying them as they, the schools, requested, not as it, the authority, commanded. The authority would, obviously, have to safeguard itself. It would have deliberately created a volatile situation of motion and invention. Its teaching force, to take a prime example, could not be viewed calmly as a quota of professionals distributed on a per capita or subject basis around the schools. The authority would have to protect teachers' pay and prospects by running its personnel side as a kind of staffing agency to which schools might turn. Cost restriction would probably do the trick indirectly, but it might be necessary for an authority to legislate for minimal and maximal staff ratios for its schools.

As now, the authority would organise supply, maintenance and other services. In the new regime, however, the decision when and how much to use such agencies would entirely depend on the localities. Occasionally, the authority might find itself arbitrating on priorities when, for instance, a couple of schools demanded to be decorated the same week, or, for that matter, persuading one school to submit to fresh decoration in an otherwise slack week. There again is a slight example of the providing agency balancing the needs of the general—the authority's—interest with the needs of the local—the school's-interest.

In other words, although teachers and parents might be denied choice of the frame, the picture would be theirs to paint as they wished. If that whole range of decisions was placed in the lap of the school community, it could make for radical improvements in the close identification of the local people with local school. It would amount to the culmination of a two-way process, whereby the school arena became less changeable, as the mixed ability, co-ed, comprehensive neighbourhood school was installed, and what happened within that arena became more changeable, as local decision-making and enforcement was dramatically extended.

It could not be left at that. The authority previously outlined its aims. At the end of the day it must somehow measure the success or failure of the endeavour to achieve them. Possibly the most topsy-turvy aspects of the topsy-turvy world of educational administration is that evaluation occurs implicitly *before* the exercise takes place, contrary to the general run of examination being retrospective. This happens probably because schooling is approached from a highly legalistic angle. The Department of Education and Science and the local education authority combine to establish a system that will provide for obedience to the law. In the knowledge that children have to be educated for so many sessions, in buildings and conditions meeting certain standards, from the age of five to sixteen, according to certain simple criteria of supervision, the system prejudges what is wanted and provides it. The assessment is a preface to the activity. Provided that the law is kept and can be kept, few other assessments are attempted. Again, one is perhaps guilty of overemphasis. Some authorities do attempt to investigate the results of their labours and those of their employees, with the assistance of reading tests and other diagnostic means.

There are inspections, by both local advisers and the national inspectorate, but these are rarely regular or precise enough to act as guide or policy. They are not perhaps intended to be. Her Majesty's

Inspectors delight in eschewing their invigilatory role, preferring the more laudable mantle of the missionary. Carrying the seeds of 'good practice' in their cross-pollination satchels, the HMIs journey hither and thither, loudly protesting that they are the teachers' best friends. Where local officers or organisers do examine the schools in their thrall, they do so tentatively and subjectively. The reputation of a school, good or bad, is too often founded on spurious and mythical legend. Parents may be impressed by the triumphant academic record obtained by children whose background made it all but impossible for them to fare badly. Conversely, they may be offended by progressive methods in the primary school which, whilst successful, they might suspect and resent. Others correlate violence in city secondary schools with comprehensive reorganisation as a hard, direct link. Teachers, like most humans, disapprove of criticism, especially of a theoretical or scientific nature. Sometimes one feels that the teachers get the credit for success and the pupils the blame for failures.

In this atmosphere, evaluation is not easy, and there is a further compounding of the difficulty. A straightforward measurement of children's academic attainment, in terms of reading ages, intelligence quotients, number tests and on to trial by external examination, is possible, and, indeed, some authorities already do some of this. But the stated aim of the system proposed here was social rather than academic, or, to be more precise, social embracing academic. The child was viewed, in Paulo Freire's telling phrases, as 'subject', active in forming his own skills and finding his own knowledge, rather than 'object', the passive recipient of information transmitted from others. Then the child was set in his communal context, as a maker of choices, as youngster and as adult..

Such activities are extremely resistant to so-called scientific research. Taking the ever-newsworthy topic of literacy, available tests might inform us that a child's reading age, by dint of a particular treatment over a certain period, had risen from 7.3 to 8.5. It has been truly remarked that the important point is not whether a child can read, but whether he does read, and with what degree of sophistication, and, further, for the community educator, whether, as adult, he continues to use his literary skills in an increasingly sophisticated manner.

Yet it is incumbent upon an authority to weigh schools in some sort of balance, in order to justify expenditure and ensure goals are attempted, if not achieved. First, three factors should be plainly spelled out to teachers, parents, children, and rate-payers alike.

1. The concept of the educative community exonerates teachers from culpability if results are unfavourable. There may, one hastens to

add, be complicity, but if the hypothesis of the total environmental effect on schooling is believed, then the teachers should not be held entirely responsible, any more than they should be adulated if children reach dizzy heights of scholastic responsibility. Once teachers are seen by everyone to enjoy the kind of immunity doctors do, in that the health condition of an area is not laid at the local general practitioner's surgery door, then education statistics might be received with the relative calm and aplomb that characterises the receipt of health statistics.

2. Everyone should likewise be clear that it is not individual children who are being examined. Such a technique may be necessary in the *internal* running of a school, and external examinations will, of course, be acknowledged individually: there is not as yet an O-level collective. But, in assessing school communities, the authority would not primarily be concerned with individual pupils. It is not the 'basic standard' children should, according to some right-wing opinion, be expected to reach. There would be no hint of stigma, nor any backward glance at selection in this. The education authority would be no more interested, externally speaking, in labelling the child whose reading was below par than the medical authority would be in publishing a list of names of those who had suffered from bronchitis in the preceding year. Thus would the children, as well as the teachers, be seen to be outside the immediate phase of investigation.

3. Evaluation would be, after all, a *quid pro quo*. This fictional, but, one hopes, not unrealistic authority has handed power over to the school communities in a dramatic and fullblooded way. It has given the schools to the communities of teachers, parents and children who use them. The authority is saying, in effect we give the schools back to the people; we have started a general aim and secured a general frame of reference; under the heading of 'local diagnosis' we entrust you with the responsibility of resolving how most effectively that general aim can be particularised and attained in your special situation; but, having done that, it is our beholden function to judge how successful that has been. In brief, local autonomy in exchange for authority evaluation seems a just swap.

What measures should be adopted to ascertain success or failure? One might suggest four areas of interpretation of a school's activity *vis-à-vis* the aims originally proposed.

1. *Academic.* It would be realistic and proper to include some academic testimony. Obviously, ratepayers expect a school to educate in the

traditional sense, and the conventional forms of schooling—literacy and numeracy—are indispensable tools in the social education programmes of community schools. Thus a sparse and none too burdensome sequence of evidence should be sought, possibly with internal testing of oral, verbal, numerical and social skills at seven and eleven, together with a reliance on external examination, such as GCE and CSE, in the higher educational reaches. But it should be stressed that this purely academic content is only a part, not even the supreme part, of the evaluative exercise. The local authority should draw up its standards, perhaps according to national averages, in the hope that all schools would meet or approach these, including, of course, remedial requirements.

2. *Social and Creative.* As a balance to this, the authority should also request evidence about the social and creative elements in the children's activities. Again, according to fairly generalised and flexible norms, each school should be judged as to the social adaptability and creative potential realised in its pupils. This would, in part, be a watch on curriculum, to ensure that its community-orientated elements and the opportunities for music, art, theatre, dance, recreations, sports, and so on (preferably, admixtures of the two) were available in some strength, and, in part, a survey of the children's developments in active social and creative skills.

3. *Parental Involvement.* Turning to the parental engagement of the school, there would be an important requirement on schools to log and report the quantity and quality of adult participation. This could cover the full spectrum from direct observation of and involvement in child-centred school-work, via the very necessary social relationships a school develops with parents, to the part played by parents and other adults in school management, and the programme of adult activities, recreational and educational, on offer.

4. *Communal Climate.* Lastly, there would be the social tone of the district, and the manner in which the school contributed to this. Various social malaise indicators might be used, particularly those directly concerning the young, such as vandalism, truancy and juvenile delinquency. Once more, according to its own lights, the authority would need to establish a norm of what it could reasonably expect of a well-balanced urban district.

Such quadruple interpretation of a school's productivity, perhaps completed annually, would be double-edged. On the one hand, it would require a school to strive for success, utilising ways and devices it had itself decided were viable, in order to preserve the continuity of its supply of funds and resources. On the other hand, because of the authority's fundamental acceptance of the total nature of the educative climate, there would, other things being equal, be no shame in failure. It would not follow, for example, that if only 10 per cent of a school's fifteen-year-olds, as opposed to the nation's 20 per cent, obtained five O-levels, that that school was, *per se*, internally disastrous; nor would, as a consequence of a high degree of graffiti or junior shoplifting in its catchment area, a school be judged a social flop. This would be the other side of the medallion: the recognition that, because of extramural factors affecting O-levels or vandalism, that school would need other or more resources.

Local diagnosis begins at authority level. It would be wooden and sterile to lay down a national evaluative frame, but, to fill out this nebulous research quartet, one or two pointers may be in order. In the academic sphere, the national averages suggest that: at seven, 70 per cent are average or above average readers; at eleven 79 per cent are; some 20 per cent or more obtain five O-levels and stay on after the school leaving age; and 7 per cent or 8 per cent move on to higher education. In the social and creative sphere, one might expect a curriculum with a 50 per cent devotion to studies of a social environment tack, together with a 25 per cent (possibly in overlap) opportunity for cultural activity in its broadest sense. Surveys of social skills and attitudes, plus a record of a school's community action and spectrum of leisure, artistic and allied offerings, would also be useful. In the parental sphere, one might expect some form of contact, however slight, on a weekly basis with every family, together with a wide programme of options for adults in the community to follow. In the communal sphere, ward rankings on social malaise indicators would be a helpful guide, as long as they were balanced with a recital of positive virtues, such as an increase in community service and involvement in the district.

An authority with this kind of information at its behest could legitimately shift and transfer resources to sustain an equal harmony. This could be the foundation for a full-run version of positive discrimination, one in which schools not only received 'more' but 'different'; that is, a literal connotation of 'discrimination', by which schools used variable techniques of their own choice, rather than just intensifications of the same techniques. Schools that could not, because of the factors in their social context, meet the set objectives, would receive greater funds and materials to deploy in the manner in which they felt success could be guaranteed. Harshly, it must by that token be recognised that those schools, where social factors appear more favourable, would obtain less support.

Such a system, even with some form of slide-rule as here envisaged, would require superb and ingenious political management. The measuring-rods could never be more than rules-of-thumb, and the idea of schools being treated unequally would produce all kinds of antagonisms and special pleadings. The line between a school trying its damnedest in a deprived district, and one cruising in a less deprived district, would take no little resoultion. The astute head or managers, realising that success could mean reduced resources, might, in some aspects (home-school relations, for instance) be prepared to keep activities just this side of the critical line. One must, alternatively, be careful not to punish imagination and flair, and there must be rather encouragement of inventive and eager experimentation. All in all, educational assessment would remain a subtle political as well as a clearcut scientific exercise. Nevertheless, if resources are to be utilised for the attainment of overall aims, there can be no retreat from such a course, however arduous and unpleasant.

At a further remove, one might hope to see the central state adopt a similar combine of positive discrimination and 'regional' or 'authority' diagnosis. If a series of general aims and a widesweeping pattern of reference could be nationally determined, then the local authorities could practise their own brand of educational management according to their own lights, subject naturally enough to some form of external investigation. This would be analogous to the local authority-community formula already outlined. Once more the hackneyed cliché of the piper and the tune needs to be modified. The piper is the state and the payers who call the tune are, or should be, the people. In other words, the state could very well finance education completely, as several commentators have suggested, from the national exchequer, provided that the local authorities might decide policy and priorities. It is the state as servant, rather than master, with the Department of Education a kind of educational corporation which (granted the overall aims and general assessment) provides as the local authority commissions and requests. Furthermore, the principle of positive discrimination could equally apply. For too long, the large conurbations and other industrial districts have accumulated the social problems of the kingdom, against an accompanying relative reduction in the revenue available for action. If one of the criteria for the distribution of funds was need, that is, the educational compensation for social factors inhibiting the attainment of educational objectives, then a major cause of educational inequality could be met. There is strong evidence of authorities with lower achievement ratios being, in alliance, areas of high working-class populations and low rating incomes.

Much of this encroaches on the later discussion of the administration of a community education system, but it was essential to relate school organisation with the establishment and measurement of objectives. The fundamental issue is equality. One must not be over-categorical, and there must, naturally, be room for manoeuvre and variety, but, if we firmly believe in equality, we should so organise our education system to produce it. To take an example, if, as is the present case, our economy seems to require and/or can only afford 7 or 8 per cent of its children to move on to higher education, then we should not expect to find, in any given non-selective group of a hundred children, too much deviation from the norm. At the moment, it varies from just over 2 per cent in one town to nearly 20 per cent in another. My view would be that such a spread makes a nonsense of any concept of equality. Unless one is prepared to adopt a draconian and spectacular view of heredity on a social class or even geographical basis, one is forced to accept that much of this gigantic variation is man-made and environmental, and thus open to reversal. While accepting that much of that man-made environment is outside the realm of the school, that is still no excuse for refusing battle, for not desperately attempting to seek out an equitable and just formula. To some this may sound like a lowering or dragging down of standards, in that it is implied that, if an authority has an inordinate amount of success, this might be stemmed. In a society where there is a limit of resources, both in personnel and materials, one must accept that, if some children are penalised by social accident, then there are some children over-favoured. The one is as unjust as the other. Obviously, one would be pleased if more opportunities were available for more children to be more highly educated for an economy which demanded more well-qualified people; and immediately one enters again an overlap phase of education and jobs and the complex question of income.

One can only hope that others are about the task of setting to rights such other features of society as employment and incomes; the education administrator must persevere, as far as possible, in providing all children with an equal chance, where 'equal' equals 'fair' and not 'uniform'. The contention is here that this could best be implemented by the authority concentrating on the strategy while leaving the tactics to the schools. If this could be parallel with a situation in which the central state concentrated on the grand strategy, and allowed the authorities to evolve the field strategies, then so much the better.

3. *School to Post-School*

Now comes the crucial question. When should 'school', as such, end? There are two strong reasons for suggesting that adolescence, which, for the sake of administrative simplicity, will be defined as the end of the third secondary year, is the crisis point.

1. We face a dilemma of increasing education as against receding adolescence. This is, it appears, partly a biological phenomenon, with, say some experts, puberty arriving early at the rate of a month a year over the last few years. Apart from this unexplained swing of the biological pendulum, there is also the social sense in which adolescence arrives earlier, with youngsters faced, through the media and in the peer-group, with issues from which, in recent generations, they may have been sheltered. Certainly there is no happy conjunction of puberty and adulthood. The social and economic characteristics of adulthood are pushed further backwards as education moves up the age-range. Over the last eighty years the school leaving age has risen from eleven to sixteen. It has casually by-passed, without so much as a by-your-leave, the most important watershed in a human's development, the onset of manhood or womanhood. Whatever cosmetic surgery we attempt on the school, it is still the agency which caters for the four- and five-year-old.

   Many secondary teachers would agree that their troubles really begin in the later years, when they struggle to encompass 'young adults' in the type of institution they had perhaps quite enjoyed as children. Indeed, as some sections of the press rage about the collapse of schools and of relations between teachers and pupils, it is always worth recalling that the rapport between teachers and primary children has probably been never happier nor more productive than at the present time.

2. By the same token, the role of the parent apropos 'the child' changes with the onset of adolescence. The parental task differs: it is not so intimately concerned with the day-by-day welfare and education of the youngster in the way that a pre-school mother's is. There are, of course, new worries and problems, but they have a slightly different base. It is not without reason that Lady Plowden has distinguished between 'parental participation' at the primary and 'parental consultation' at the secondary level. There is a natural growth away from the parent as adolescence approaches, and, more

positively, the parent is also re-emerging from the close child-attachment role of those earlier years. The parent, too, is becoming an adult in his or her own right, with new educational needs. Of course, the parent has always had 'adult' educational needs, and, for many parents, as one child reaches puberty, there are one or two more, so to speak, in the pipeline. But, in terms of each one-to-one correspondence, the mood changes from the intense parent-child to the looser adult-young adult relationship.

As this transition occurs, the parent-child-teacher triangle, which is the keystone of the community school, changes also. Many would unhappily testify to the difficulty of piloting the kind of home-school relations in secondary schools which have prospered in primary schools.

For these two compelling reasons there is a sound case for defining the community school as the educational *locus* for children up to the third secondary year, that is, fourteen plus. In a brief and simple phrase, school is for children. All that has been so far said about the school, about its objectives, about its tactics and about its assessment, should be seen in the novel regard of the school ending at fourteen.

This would make for an enormous reorientation. An initial practical difficulty would be buildings. For many, many years, until an ambitious building programme could be negotiated, the authority would need to rely on existing premises. It might not be easy to develop five-to-fourteen schools on single sites. In advocating what some may dub as a return to the 'all-age' school, one should recollect that the major argument for abandoning the all-through school was inadequate facilities for older children, and no one would wish to see a retrogression to that situation. There might be some need to retain a transfer of bodies at eleven-plus or thereabouts, but this need not deter us. Indeed one should look for the advantages, and three swiftly spring to mind.

1. The distinction at fourteen-plus would mean a much closer fluidity from the feeder primary school to the new lower secondary stage. In some parts of many authorities, one might envisage a *First* (i.e. infant/junior) and a *Second* (i.e. first three years of present secondary) school. A closer connection would apply to staff, curriculum, resources and—in terms of specialist equipment—children. One would try to ensure a unity of progress and process for the whole of the age-range from starting school to adolescence. It is assuredly a unity at present lacking, as secondary teachers claim their primary colleagues do not 'prepare' their charges adequately, and

the primary staffs counter with the view that their secondary confrères fail to build properly on the work they have accomplished.

2. The distinction at fourteen-plus would allow for the kind of schedule already planned in some progressive secondary schools, namely a child-centred, flexible approach by class-teaching or, preferably, team-teaching of mixed ability groups in the initial three years. The points so far inferred about life-related curricula, about active, not passive, education, about the recognition of the place of the home in that education: all these would apply upward. The departmental and specialist subject teaching would evolve into the child-centred study of socially relevant themes and skills, as in the more community-orientated primary and middle-schools now operating. That strange division, in some secondary schools of 'pastoral' and 'academic' duties would end. The idea that one teacher caters for the social and another for the intellectual nature of the child is to carry the artificial divorcement of education from its social context right into the very heart of the classroom.

   One example of a solution would be, say, for a dozen mixed specialists to greet two hundred and fifty eleven-year-olds and arrange with them a three-year programme of activities. The permutations then become less exhaustible. One might for a session, take two hundred and the other eleven split the remaining fifty into small tutorial groups. A joint venture over a period of weeks or months would be possible, as over against the curfew tolling the knell of parting periods. Here again, however, the principle of local diagnosis must be urged. It would be the task of the teachers and parents of the five-to-fourteen school to meet the agreed aims in their own fashion. It would be their responsibility to guarantee that each youngster would enjoy a smooth and continuous appraisal of his essential childhood, set against its community context.

3. The distinction at fourteen-plus would be a natural one, but, because of the present division into, basically, tiny primaries and huge secondaries, it would be necessary to align a series of feeder primaries with each secondary school. In turn, the essential unity of approach would lend substance to the very idea of 'feeder' schools, for, at present, the distinction at eleven-plus is not only a misleading and synthetic one, it is also an overweighty one. The child moves abruptly from a small class-based location to a large subject-based location.

Each authority and indeed each community would need to make its own adjustments, as architectural, as well as educational, determinants suggested. One possibility would be to use the lower school facilities of a secondary school as a specialist centre for its local primary feeders. For instance, take a secondary school of 1,500, with an 8-form intake of 240. This would represent, for its first 3 years, space for 720 children. If this school had 8 feeder primaries, contributing 30 pupils each a year, then those 8 schools, presumably with rolls of about 180 apiece, could provide for a 5-14 register of 270, as long as, at any one time, any 90 of them were using the centralised facilities of the secondary school (i.e. $90 \times 8 = 720 =$ the space theoretically available in the first three years). Seasoned time-tablers might pale at the logistics to which that premiss would commit them, but it could be one interim answer to continuous schooling. An ideal solution, of course, would be, say, 5 purpose-built schools for groups of 430 pupils for the 2,150 children hypothesised in this arithmetical conundrum.

The authority posited as a kind of Aunt Sally for this exercise contains some 32,000 children in the five-to-fourteen age group, spread over 90 primary schools and the early years of 15 secondary schools. An ideal answer would be 60 brand-new schools of 500 or so youngsters. In practice, the association of roughly 4 to 8 primary schools with each of the 15 secondary schools would prove to be the most efficient solution, giving the authority something like 15 tightly meshed groups of, approximately, 7 community schools of this novel type.

4. Post-school

This proposal of the adolescent watershed next leads to a reconsideration of the post-school, that is, post-fourteen education stage. The motif is adulthood. The idea is that the young adult may fare more happily moving towards an 'adult' educational sphere rather than being held back in a child-based one. It was interesting and rather sad, during the ROSLA experiments, to hear school-leavers admit that the new curriculum programmes were more interesting, but that colleges of further education, whatever their shortcomings of syllabus, were more comfortable places to be. The atmosphere was more adult. It was laughable to hear some head teachers call for 'relevant, positive, interesting and realistic' activities in the ROSLA year; one could hardly forbear to wonder why the same emphasis was not considered necessary in the first few years of secondary schooling. Still, the authority must obey the law of the land and assure full-time education until sixteen.

There is, nevertheless, no encumbrance placed on the agency which so provides, and the adult-orientation calls for the development of the *community college*, as the proper extension and completion of the institutional system of community education. It would be both adjunct to and successor of the five-to-fourteen community school.

It is not particularly a revolutionary statement. It resurfaces the 'county college' clause enshrined in the 1944 Act, but rarely implemented, and it tries to fit it to the 1970s and 80s. In practice it would be founded in the existing further education colleges, or in the upper parts of the existing secondary schools, those higher echelons not utilised by the preceding school. Naturally, there would be spatial interplay: the children would not preclude their elders from the only gym, or find themselves denied the library by their encroaching elder brothers and sisters. Again, this is not an unfavourable point. The adjoined presence of 'school' and 'college', and the opportunity for interflow between them, could be a distinct advantage as compared with some further education practice.

It could, for example, permit of a phased transition at thirteen or fourteen of our new-type 'school-leaver'. If adolescence is the key to transfer, then it does not arrive instantaneously; and thus the move from school to college, to complete one's full-time education, could profitably be cautious and slow. One hesitates at some kind of puberty trial, reminiscent of the chromosome tests of the Olympic Games; maybe if teacher, parent and child could somehow arrive at a consensus view of the optimal time of transfer, then everyone's interests would be served.

The essential point about the community college would be that it should offer a full-run educational service to all adults, that is, post-adolescents, in a given community. These would range from the rising fifteen-year-old teenager, serving out his obligatory educational period, to the old age pensioner, looking for social activity and cultural solace.

Each community would be left to plan its own collegiate operation, but the options on offer might include:

1. *Academic.* This would be for O- and A-level, CSE and other external examinations. The fourteen-plus transfer allows for the necessary two-year course for O-level or CSE exams. It is likely that the three-year grounding in educational activity and skills of a life-related kind described earlier would form a firmer foundation for an assault on examinations than the often dulling, repetitive stages of that false defence of stale academy, the 'accumulative' subject. It is hoped that, by retaining the curiosity and extending the aptitude of

each child, then, by fourteen, the motivation might be enhanced so that sheer academic performance would be lifted. More importantly, it is felt that, given that mind-widening experience for both parent and child, the actuality of choice, of whether to take examinations and which ones to take, would be a richer and more studied decision. Incidentally, one might also expect to see a continuation of the present pleasing trend in 'local diagnosis' for syllabuses, as in CSE Mode III.

2. *Vocational and Professional.* Such courses would be, as now, for jobs, trades and careers. They are especially important in urban areas where under-employment is a facet of economic life. With rapid changes in the technology of our economic fabric and the consequent recycling of work-patterns, the need for vocational aid, not once, but possibly several times during a person's working life, grows ever more urgent. Here, once more, is a sphere where upper secondary and further education already share the workload. A combined operation could be that much more effective.

3. *Social and Communal.* Such programmes would be planned for participation in and preparation for life in society as citizens, voters, consumers, workers and so on. By now the child has grown into man or woman, and the community college would be the forge for the welding and refining of adult action in the community. It would be expected that practice would illustrate precept. The college would be the focus for community action. It might house the editorial offices and printing presses of the community newspaper.

   A good example might be preparation for parenthood courses. These might entail the college being directly involved in the co-ordinated pre-school policy previously envisaged. The adults obtaining assistance in early childhood training might be, as parents, crucially concerned in many of the district's pre-reception units. This is an interesting instance of the circular nature of community education with the community college promoting adult education of a kind helpful to the sustenance of pre-school education.

4. *Cultural and Recreational.* The college would normally offer a wide spectrum of sports, arts, crafts, leisure pursuits, hobbies and re-creations, all of them contributing so much to the quality of individual, family and communal life. In the event, the college would be well-placed to be the fulcrum for much community activity. It could be a meeting-place, a centre for sporting competitions or dramatic performances, and so on. The linkages with other associations and clubs in the neighbourhood could, at these junctures, be close and plentiful.

But the most powerful difference would lie in the adult togetherness, signs of which are now to be seen in secondary schools up and down the country. A sixteen-year-old might find him or herself studying O-level biology with a mature student, anxious to take up teacher-training; or electrical engineering with tradesmen on day release courses; or the problems of work with budding shop stewards or trainee managers; or the pleasures of film-making with an old age pensioner. This might, among other things, be beneficial in solving some of the 'problems' of adolescence as now defined. The incorporation of teenagers with older adults in working groups might very well temper some of the friction and antagonism engendered by the present strain of teachers of children in confrontation with 'adult pupils'.

All this, of course, notes the demise of further education as a separate tertiary administrative entity. It would, alternatively, invite a co-ordinated response from all purveyors of adult education at present deployed haphazardly throughout the towns and cities. Thus an authority, or the appropriate governing body of a community college, might invite organisations like the Workers Educational Association, the Open University and the University Extra-Mural Departments to co-operate in dovetailing their resources and expertise. Naturally, the authority's colleges of further education and, where applicable, its polytechnic would be drawn completely into this new format. A polytechnic might well stand at the apex of the community college pyramid, a crowning glory of the system, providing a central source of highly specialised facilities and courses to each of its brethren at district level. The evening institutes and the youth service of the authority would logically be drafted into this co-ordinated whole.

Local diagnosis would be required yet once more, as each college endeavoured to meet the prior and overall needs of its catchment community, responding sympathetically to the pulse-beat of that area. Educational demands are varied and legion, and, through a constant and fluent intercommunion of all community colleges, an authority-wide nexus of opportunities could be made available. The community college, like the community school before it, would be subject to community control and to authority assessment, together with that same carefully weighed practice of positive discrimination for the provision of funds and resources.

It would not be an inward-looking institution. It would be the centre for outgoing activities, taking education out to the workplace and shopping precinct, as well as attracting people physically into the college. Its quantitative aim would be high: nothing less than making some contact with as many adults in its community as could be managed. This interlacing of all adult educational, social and cultural ventures, statutory and voluntary, is not unlike the approach suggested for a co-operative attack on the pre-school problem. It carries with it the same shift in style and the same emphasis on suiting the ethos and substance of the agency to the cultural demands and patterns of the people in the community. As at differing times and in differing ways, the pub and the church have offered people a natural focal point, so must now the community school and the community college seize the opportunity to promote an affinity with its customers at once appropriate and lively.

Chapter 8

The Administrative Framework

COMMUNITY CONTROL

The institutional line—pre-school, community school (four/five to thirteen/fourteen), community college—meets the chronological point, and provides a mesh of agencies which could, vitally and properly organised, narrow the huge gaps at present existing in educational provision. In narrowing the chasm one would also expect to see a change in aim, or, at least, in emphasis, as schools and colleges concentrated more on turning out a product capable of effective choice than on instilling ready-tailored choices.

An authority planning such a radical alteration in the objectives and fabric of its educational service would need to look as critically at its administrative mechanics, the weft, as it were, interwoven with the institutional warp. Two considerations would be uppermost, before such an appraisal commenced. They would relate back to the two basic dilemmas described in Chapter 5, namely the conflict of representative as opposed to popular control, and the latent contest between professional and layman. It is proposed to examine each in turn, whilst not forgetting their intrinsic relation.

1. *The Community 'Constituency'*

The school and college, reformed along lines of individual choice with a community orientation, could rightly be seen as an important aspect of community development and the movement towards a participatory democracy. It is arguable that the school is the lowest common denominator of community life, in that everyone has been or is at school, everyone lives near a school, everyone, in rates or taxes, supports schools, and often one has or had a child at school. If the teacher is a representative of the authority *vis-à-vis* the citizenry, then he is, for the majority, the most familiar and easily-recognised representative. He is the front-of-house man for the authority, and many teachers could fill out that description with anecdotes of their social roles embracing much from ministering angel to private eye.

There is also the important issue, already discussed, that school and college do indirectly, and should more directly, service all the other community processes. This might mean the straightforward business of voting for councillors, or the more complicated procedures of coping adequately with the intricacies of local bureaucracy or of contributing manfully to one's tenants' association or trade union.

The educated person is one who, armed with social skills and competences, is the better able to make *informed* choices about the destiny of himself, his family and his community or communities. This is a circle of argument. One of the communal aspects about which choices must be made is, of course, education. The citizen, in that ring of development, would make more informed choices about the system which enabled him to make more informed choices about the system . . . and so on.

Nor is there any reason for delay. Some might claim that, until a reformed educational process had produced this perfect citizen, then he should not be let loose upon it. It is a trifle patronising, however, to see the situation in that way. The citizenry are, quite evidently, by no means devoid of the common sense and competences to examine the system quizzically. Indeed, the wheel already revolves, in that more and more people, over the last hundred years, have had more and more education, and, by dint of that both as an experience in itself and as a provider of skills, the lay expertise is by no means sparse. What is plainly lacking is knowledge, especially about the manner in which the educational process occurs and in which educational attainment is produced. One must, conversely, not be too dewy-eyed: information has a nasty habit of reinforcing prejudice and of being interpreted according to preconception. However, it is fair to suggest that so-called progressive tendencies— modern primary school method, the ideology and practice of comprehension, the relation of education to social context, curricular reform, and a number of other features—have never been concisely and vividly portrayed to the public.

In any event, the alternative is arrogant and autocratic. The parents and children use the schools and the rate and tax-payers pick up the tab. To deny them a major share in the control of one of the nation's largest industries, and one that affects, at some stage, the entire population, would be as foolish as it would be criminal. It is not cynicism that suggests we should educate our masters. Social provision, it must be emphasised, operates in interlock: to be well-to-do, to be healthy, to be law-abiding, to be educated, each is a part of the other. In that it operates as a set of public services, social provision is of the people and must, in all conscience, work at their behest.

Given in such and such a district, a community college, with feeder community schools, with their pre-school annexes, then there must be a stout case for devolving much of the decision-making and resources control to that level. It is well known that this form of district control is being canvassed now in several local authorities and for several services. This analysis is not an attempt at novelty, but at synthesis, at pulling into some kind of shape the implications of many existing tendencies towards community devolution. One meaningful factor to be borne in mind is the case for education, devolved to district level, being but a fraction of an overall or interdisciplinary attack by all local services. One of the prime concerns of community management would be to ensure that the lines of bureaucracy would not be cast separately from town hall and arrive, at district level, in a vexed tangle.

It may well be that education is in the strongest bargaining position to promote such delegation of powers to community level. Be that as it may, it would be most profitable if all the forces of social provision could be developed on cross-disciplinary lines. The premier considerations would be health and welfare, not only medical, but spilling over into the positive spheres of housing and environmental quality; the police and other law and order concerns, such as a local magistracy and probation service; and social services, again stressing not only the maintenance of income through state benefits but less negative aspects like local employment opportunities. The best of the nineteenth century might combine with the best of the twentieth. The concept of the Local Board of Health, the district School Board, the borough Watch Committee, and the Board of Guardians showed promise of district vigour and autonomy; but they were stultified by Victorian crassness, prejudice, haphazardness, austerity, and they never became rationalised into holistic approaches. In a freer and more democratic clime, localised services, operating in the same relatively small territorial pale, could be a necessary counter to the impersonal administrative hugeness with which the twentieth century resolved the problems posed by the sporadic and illogical attempts of the nineteenth century.

It would be a happy conjunction if these smaller areas could be aligned with the political ward boundaries. This would mean that another pleasing interface would be found, that of town or city government and community bounds. There would be obvious advantages if the electoral and official areas were co-identified.

The district community should be judged in historical and geographical terms, as well as by sheer space and numbers. Where possible, existing 'natural' environs should be retained. There are still many districts which, however tenuously, cling to a sense of togetherness, even if only in a name or an activity. This organic sense of local organisation, often sadly lacking in the 1974 local government reorganisation, could be crucial in any attempts at popular government. Of course, size of population and area must count, but the natural determinants should be followed where possible.

Approaching the issue merely from an educational angle, one might foresee an educational district based on one or a small group of secondary schools, the upper part or parts of which would form the newly-proposed community college, together with the appropriate series of feeder community schools and pre-reception units. Hopefully, such a catchment community could be viably aligned with the kind of political and official unison suggested.

In outlining the institutional framework for education a double loop of administration was envisaged, which can be simply summarised in the accompanying diagram. Concentrating on the authority-district dichotomy, one might anticipate the establishment of democratic control. The important point is the identification of control with function.

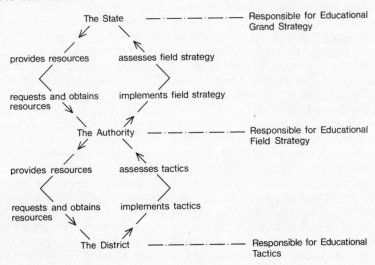

Devolution of control gives the people (teachers, parents, adult students, perhaps children) using an institution a real chance of running it according to the needs and demands, the strengths and weaknesses, of the local situation. Especially if this were related to other community-based services, they would be able more competently to measure local problems and available resources, against the financial and general policy enunciated by the education committee of the authority. This is not a diminution of the committee's responsibility. It would rather relieve the education committee of some of the purely localised issues and decisions which constantly face it and bog it down in small-scale arguments and debates, or else, which is as bad, render it a mere rubber-stamping body, unable fully to grasp the detail of the multifarious fragments placed before it in copious committee papers. Delegation to district level could allow the education committee the scope to examine, deeply and broadly, the character of educational provision for the authority in general, concentrating on its deployment of resources, its assessment techniques and its profesional infrastructure, of which more in the second section of this chapter.

There would be, then, a *community education board*. This would, in turn, entail a vertical and not a horizontal official structure. A vitally important main headquarters or secretariat would remain, but, from that hub, the administration would project, in unified form, to identify with both the clientele and the professional teaching force at the point of functional impact. Thus each district or community would house its own *community education officer* and he would enjoy a relatively complete grasp of that district's educational situation, apropos staffing, maintenance, relations with the public, resources, equipment, materials and finance. In most authorities the categories of administration are by 'service', that is, there is a supplies section or a staffing section. In this reformed context, the only category would be 'community'.

Put another way, the community education officer, and his staff, would act rather like a bursar or registrar for the community college and its allied schools in each district. He would be the chief officer to the education board, and, like that body, he would work to and from the general principles elaborated by the authority education department. As far as possible the devolution of services would follow the devolution of power, so that the community education officer's staff would include officers competent in the varied requirements of educational administration, such as salaries, equipment, repairs, meals and so forth. In some cases an authority might regard it as expedient to centralise one or another category of administration. Economies of scale, with regard to expensive machinery or rarely used specialists, might dictate this. When this occurred, the emphasis would be on the provision of service to the community education board as and when it required it.

The critical characteristic would be the singularity of administrative contact for the parents and teachers running the schools and colleges. Instead of the exhausting pursuit from the pillar of one section to the post of another in order to discover who will meet which need, the lay-professional controlling group would relate, directly and absolutely, to one executive focus. Many teachers and managers and parents will testify to the difficulties of connecting the field-level problems and issues of a school with the seemingly far away fastnesses of the authority's office and officers. The ensuing ritual of chasing the buck is not unlike some ancient and complicated folk-dance, save that it seems not to be guided by a wish for fertility or productivity. There would seem to be, and not only in education but throughout the spectrum of social provision, an urgent case for closing the gap between executive back-up and the actual function planned. The community education officer would, at the very least, provide a clearing-house for the administrative support demanded by the community college and schools in his district.

The community education board would be a cross between a district education committee and a board of management for the local college and its attendant schools and pre-schools. It would consist of at least one councillor, particularly if he was a member of the authority education committee; elected teachers and parents; locally co-opted members; and students (now it will be recalled, all post-fourteen) of the community college. It would be essential to guarantee that, among the parents and teacher delegates, there was sufficient representation of the community school tier. Another consideration would be the form of election. The recent trend in parent governors has been disappointing in terms of interest shown. In some communities this may stem from a reluctance to attend a dry, formal meeting at 7.30 p.m. on a Tuesday evening. Part of the autonomy permitted each district would be scope to evolve the forms of popular recruitment appropriate to its district culture. Postal ballot, door-to-door canvas, elections conjoined with social occasions, teasing out representatives from class groups of parents and then drafting a school representation from these, and so on.

Let us take the comparatively simple example of an area with a community college, plus an upper community school (the lower school of the one secondary school in the district, now reorganised) with say, six feeder departments and a related pattern of pre-schooling. Then the community education board might comprise:

(a) The community education officer.

(b) A local councillor, preferably one with membership of the authority education committee.

(c) Post-school organiser, i.e. head of community college and its offshoots.

(d) Schools organiser, i.e. head of the community school structure.

(e) Pre-school organiser for that district.

(f) Teacher representative from the college, the upper school and for the six feeders, say, four delegates.

(g) Parent representatives similarly for the upper school and six feeders, plus one for pre-school (four).

(h) All-age student representatives for the community college (four).

Total: seventeen, plus any co-opted members.

A number of points should be noted. First, each separate entity—the college, the different school bases, the pre-school set-up—would have its own committee, similar to the present boards of governors or managers, except that parents, teachers and (in the case of the college) students would be the chief participants on an elective basis. Second, the education board would normally be composed of parents and teachers already serving on the smaller committees. Given, as in this standard case, ten or eleven separate bases, it would be over-weighty to have teachers and parents from each. It would, therefore, be important that all should speak in the appointments to the larger board. For instance, the parent members on all the school committees could meet to elect their four representatives under (g) above. Some areas may wish to designate by age-range, for instance one upper school, two 'school' and one pre-school age; similarly with the teacher representation. Third, the board, in turn, would nominate a representative for the authority's new-style education committee, as apart from the local councillor. Thus would the flow of popular rule run upwards and downwards as fluidly as possible. Fourth, a significant implication of this programme would be in the role of head teacher. Logically, if there were an organiser or principal for the whole gamut of post-fourteen education (namely, the community college) and an organiser for the under-fives phase, then there should be one director of the entire school-age range, from five to fourteen, called here, in the interests of simplicity, the schools organiser. More of this anon: suffice it to remark that the smooth unification of all endeavours for schoolchildren in the district would necessitate this type of professional oversight, irrespective of the actual sites involved.

The outcome of these major shifts in the administrative order may best be delineated in the accompanying diagram:

A PROPOSED ORGANISATIONAL STRUCTURE

Education Committee

(Councillors, co-opted members, etc., with one councillor, at least, from each 'ward' or 'district' and some representation, both lay and professional from 'district' or 'community' level, responsible, as now for the overall city-wide educational policy.)

Education Department

(Organising overall planning and administration, supervising city-wide exercises [training, city-based institutions, etc.], overseeing finance, resources and services and ensuring a proper balance of priorities and achievements area to area.)

Community College

(One in each 'district' or 'community' as outlined with a post-school organiser and staffing as appropriate.)

'Community' Education Board — — *'Community' Education Office*

(A kind of district education committee-cum-board of governors for the community college, with councillors, teachers, parents, locally co-opted or elected members, students (now all post-fourteen) and representations of 'community school' tier. In concert with 'community' education office, the board would, within the city committee framework, formulate and have oversight of local policy and administration.)

(Responsible, with considerable delegated powers, along with the appropriate board, for the administration of education in that locality; powers to include finance and resources as much as possible. A further important role would be to act as an *advisory* unit for parents and other members of the local community. All under control of a *'community' education officer*.)

Community Schools

(The group of pre-school units [with a pre-school co-ordinator] and community schools feeding into the community college, with an overall schools organiser.)

'Community' School Management

(The pre-school sector and the

schools would require boards of management [parents, teachers, etc.] with powers delegated to them from the community, board of education, and in turn sending representatives to that board. It might, according to grouping, be possible to have *one* such management group for the community.)

Turning to the education committee for the model authority of 300,000 people, something like 15 communities of 20,000 could be fashioned. Each could be the equivalent of both a political ward and a community college catchment area. The education committee might then consist of fifteen councillors, one for each ward or 'community', the fifteen community education officers, representing officer and teacher opinion, and fifteen nominees from the lay members of each education board, which, with the authority's chief officers and representatives of the teachers' unions would give an education committee of some fifty-five members.

At the officer level, it might be sensible to have, in an authority, a chief education officer, backed by three co-ordinators, namely the pre-school co-ordinator, one for community schools and one for the collegiate structures. They would, respectively, relate to each community's pre-school, schools and post-school organisers. There might be other overall officers of an administrative nature or, in the case of a polytechnic or other large college, of an academic nature.

But one reservation must be firmly laid. The lesson of administrative history sorrowfully teaches of a most fertile procreation of officers and agents. It must be steadfastly sustained that this is a *transfer* of administration from a vertical to a horizontal structure, and not an augmentation. Although the central office would still remain a vital and, in some ways, more profound hub, the actual staffing would be expected to decrease abruptly, as the migration to the peripheral districts was negotiated. It should be established, as a working rule, that the number of people and the amount of money expended should not be expected to rise—one might even look for small savings. Admittedly, it would require a short period to phase out and replace or to reorientate officialdom, but, apart from this, one must press sturdily for a severe method of birth-control on administrative reproduction.

There would be wide variation from community to community, as from authority to authority. The illustrations are no more than possible examples. It is the principle that must remain sovereign and constant. The principle maintains the need for the *co-identification of governed and governor at the optimum point of function.* An authority of 300,000 souls, an authority of the size and shape established in 1974, is analogous with a small nation. There are, in fact, nation-states no larger than our big conurbations. Such an authority, if it is fortunate, will have a unity and a general pattern of behaviour and values, but it is at a much lower level where the real-life business actually happens and effects the man, woman and child in the street. The everyday business of education is about families and the schools they use. The fulcrum of local government is the lay control-professional organisation combine. The closer this can be associated with that real-life action, the more effective that combine is likely to be. Details aside, what is required is a linked sequence of that dualism of layman and officer, from the smallest school or pre-school base to the top echelons of the authority; and, beyond that, the central state. Technically, this 'linked sequence' is the seminal aspect of community development at large, and, historically, it represents an evolutionary and natural trend, rather than a topsy-turvy and synthetic construction.

An authority devolved in this manner to serve and control the requirements of a new-style community education system offers the best chance of harmonising the economies of scale and the other strengths of a large governmental unit (the authority ruling a city, a series of townships, or a rural expanse) with the localised demands and enthusiasms of a day-by-day, organic focal point (the community).

2. *The Professional Factor*

Hopefully, a decentralised authority, matching function and popular control, would help to resolve the first basic dilemma of equating democratic oversight with the large-scale service. Talk of committees and boards is always dulling and dreary, and it has little of the, perhaps superficial, excitement and colour of revolutionary ardour. Aneurin Bevan, no flaccid character himself, warned of the 'meretricious glamour' of the 'adventurous' society, and, conversely, sharpened our thinking to the 'quiet contentment' of the purportedly 'dull' society. 'The philosophy of democratic socialism', he said, 'is essentially cool in temper'.

Much of what most of us regard as stable and fair in our society was hewn solidly and has been as indefatigably preserved by sheer hard work on committees and by other methods of public debate and decision-making. There is no substitute for this, and those who shout nebulously for 'community development' should be prepared for its intensive practice. A colleague of Aneurin Bevan's, Emanuel Shinwell, has said that, when ordered to nationalise the coal-mines in the immediate post-war era, there were—after all those years of campaigning—no plans available for actually performing that grand act. Community developers and community educators should beware that pitfall, and prepare in favourable anticipation.

Of course there is no need for monotonous and tedious management and activity. One of the reasons for 'local diagnosis' is to suit education to the subculture it serves, and one of the yardsticks should be to guarantee that it is lively, vivid and compelling. This must vary according to taste and inclination, but, in searching for an educational substance which is an integral part of normal, humdrum life, it would be folly to eschew the pleasure and fascination that should characterise any educational process.

This is largely a question of style, and much of the responsibility would devolve on to the professional officer and teacher. Certain implicit job-remits have already been included by dint of describing a management formula. These could be shown by the following bureaucratic family tree:

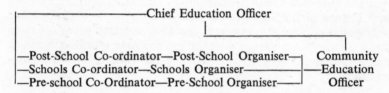

This means, in the first place, a tight, tiny inner cabinet at the top. It means in the second place, the close relationship of that high-level secretariat with those critical appointments, the community education officers. These need to be men and women of flair and verve, capable of drive and some quality of leadership, and able to find that most delicate of balances, a compromise of conceptual grasp and practical ingenuity. Obviously, the success or failure of the scheme would, to a large extent, revolve around them.

In the third place, the role of the schools organiser could be at major variance with most existing practice. The idea of one pre-school overlord and one further and adult education overlord is not a startling notion, and few would quibble with this. What might raise a few eyebrows is the concept of an organiser for a community, an overlord for the five-to-fourteen age-group. It would be, however, imperative to attain some measure of unity of purpose. This would replace the present practice in many authorities of an advisory service, sometimes torn between a general concern for a sizeable area, and a particular specialism, sometimes with a purely specialist role. Although organisers would retain something of this latter concern, the emphasis now would rather be on the task of professional development for a coherent group of schools.

Some authorities are already pioneering something of this policy, and, like so many other educational reforms, it requires educationists of, regrettably, all too rare quality to implement the idea. The authority-based advisory group has frequently grown remote and spasmodic. The sense of union of parents, children and teachers all working in the same community (with, of course, co-ordinated patterns of pre-school and post-school programmes fore and aft) would be the prior task of this school organiser.

Naturally enough, these three teams each of (to return to our sample authority) fifteen organisers would form their own networks for cross-the-board, highly specialised and task-force exercises in professional development. Nonetheless, as a trio in each area, their prime job would be to support the community education officer in constructing a novel educational format for their district.

The rapport of these organisers with the schools would need to be a fine mix of the brave and the sympathetic. The five-to-fourteen school has much logic and commonsense on its side, but, of all the themes suggested here, it could cause the most friction. To take our fictional district again, with its lower secondary school and its given eight feeder primaries, there would, presumably, be the equivalent of a head teacher in executive charge of each. The pressing requirement, however, would be for joint activity to satisfy the pledge of a unified front. Although there would be, presumably, seven, eight or more sites, the logistics needs must begin with the fact of 2,000 children and approximately 100 teachers. The schools organiser would be responsible for deploying these 100 teachers as a coherent and flexible force, and for directing the utilisation of all the premises in a beneficent manner. The fatal temptation would be to continue some form of before and after eleven schooling, especially with the need (in this case) of using the old secondary school's facilities. Once embarked, however, on a five-to-fourteen policy, it would be important to sustain the smooth momentum of that course of action.

Over a period of time, new 'schools' and 'colleges' would be constructed, deliberately geared to the new purposes and policies, probably alongside other types of allied facility to form a true all-purpose community campus. In the interim, architecture would be one of the chief stumbling-blocks, and it would be the duty of the schools organiser to moderate the severity of that hurdle. It would indeed be a key post. Of course the example quoted here, while typical, is not exclusive. For instance, an area with two secondary schools might decide to devote one to pre-fourteen and one to post-fourteen activity, and so forth. In some districts a closely-knitted mesh of a few schools might lead to a situation in which one could speak accurately of but one community school for the area, and so it would be negotiated, according to whatever compromise of buildings, personnel, local needs and overall policy could be found.

Eventually the whole ideology will live and die at the hands of the teacher. One might be lucky enough to uncover a bright and talented community education officer, together with three alert and gifted organisers. That still leaves, on average, 150 teachers. There is no point in pretending that, without their willing and eager support, all the most carefully planned structures would be of trivial avail. A community schools system requires community school-teachers. I would see it as one of the foremost tasks of the authority's education department to find these or develop their own brand.

First of all, one must consider the underlying foundations of the new professional relationship. The teacher, it was proposed, would be the steward or convener of the total *educative community*. The complete infrastructure both of schools and committees and other agencies has had this theme constantly in view. The complete system is an attempt to guide and channel the substance of that educative community. It was opined that the chasm between professional teacher and lay parent or citizen should be narrowed, by a partial 'deprofessionalisation' of the former and the concurrent professionalisation of the latter.

Examined formally, this professional underpinning of the educative community has two main elements:

1. *The community-orientated or socially-based curriculum.* This would be designed to give children and, at collegiate level, the social skills, competence and knowledge to understand their environment and their society more fully, more compassionately and more effectively. This, of course, would not entail purely local studies, for universal topics—advertising, television—are just as much a part of the child's environment and culture. Each school would need to face this curriculum issue independently, but there would be a strong argument favouring the development of resources, materials and training at both area and authority stages.

2. *The parent-child-teacher triangle.* This would affirm the dramatic effect of the home on education and the fact that education must be seen increasingly as family-based, with the teacher viewing child-plus-parent as his or her customer. Certainly if we want to make good the imbalances in educational attainment, irrespective of how we judge these, then a crucial factor would be to improve the ability of parents to support their children's education. It is reiterated that home-school relations are not just about pleasant links with parents, but about raising educational productivity. This throws an enormous burden on teachers, as presently trained, for it gives them the joint role of adult—as well as child—tutor.

It will be recalled that the diagram on organisational structure in the first section of this chapter (p. 131) called upon the community education officer to include an advisory unit for parents and others as a part of his job-specification. By promoting a broad-ranging scale of adult activities, one would likewise hope to raise the general rate of educational and social awareness.

These are but two faces of the same animal. A syllabus founded on the communal culture and a teaching relationship sought with the communal culture is near enough the same. The ideal curriculum is one in which parents can become confidently involved and make an honest contribution, and when this happens it is the ideal home-school rapport. With each learning and each teaching, the parent-child-teacher triangle becomes an equilateral one. They would echo the slogan of a previously close-knit trio, the Three Musketeers, with their 'one for all and all for one'.

A structural prerequisite of this new type of professionalism would be that of the 'extended school'. Schools and colleges would be 'extended' in two ways. On the one hand, they would be extended in the sense of hours, to meet the demands of the parents for active involvement, and to provide the communal facilities for children, parents and other adults in the evenings, at weekends and during holidays. Some of these activities have been spasmodically practised, but, in many instances, there have been separate lines of control as between school hours and evening activities or between term-time and vacations. It must be emphasised that this is nothing less than the school and its staff being constantly at the centre of an all-round, year-round service for its host community.

On the other hand, the school and the college would also be 'extended' in the sense of moving out into and mobilising that host community. It would carry the message of education to natural focal points in the community, and, in particular, to the home. Each school or teaching-team would require some 'slack' of staff, either through the medium of an education visitor or a home-school liaison teacher or through a staffing complement which enabled all or most teachers to develop such techniques.

The sum total of both these interpretations of the 'extended' school would be a tall increase in staffing, together with a more effective use of clerical, technical, caretaking and other categories of ancillary assistance. There would need to be, over the years, a more graceful acceptance of parental involvement and help, not in the sense of a dilution of professional standards, but rather by way of a rise in status, as the teacher came to be regarded as educational mentor for the entire community. Sessional timetables would be introduced, with, for example, teachers working 'ten' sessions of a 'fifteen' session week, somewhat after the fashion of further education institutions at the present.

There is no gainsaying that this would be the major increase in sheer expenditure. Much of the rest of this series of reforms requires shifts in the allocation of resources and responsibility and, more meaningfully, shifts in attitudes. But a full-run community education system, providing a cradle-to-grave service, hoping to attract many, many parents and adults as well as meeting the statutory obligation to the children, would necessitate weighty extra staffing. Let us return for a moment to the sample authority which has assisted us through this enquiry. At the moment it would, for its five-to-fourteen population, have about 1,500 (100 in each district) teachers. For the post-fourteen group, it would have only 400 (25 in each district) teachers, but one might daringly assume the existence of, say, three colleges of further education in the authority with a staff of perhaps 60 apiece. These two teams, in sum totalling about 600, would be the care of the post-fourteen adult worker, but, of course, it would be hoped that many of the actual school-teachers would (as, of course, they do now in play-centres and evening institutes) contribute heavily to extra-mural activities, especially those emanating from or meeting the demands of their own pupils' parents. Then, of course, there is the pre-school aspect, and our model authority would be fortunate to have fifty nursery teachers and nursery nurses *in situ*. With at least one pre-school assistant for every primary school under-fives as proposed in part one of Chapter 7, plus full-time help for a pattern of work perhaps affecting maybe sixty or eighty three- and four-year-olds, there would be a call for a hundred or more pre-school helpers. Bearing in mind all these elements, the total teaching force for the authority would grow, at a rough estimate, from 2,200 to 2,600 at present figures. This would allow for a teaching force of about 170 in an average community.

This is unavoidable. For too long the pioneer and experimental work in these areas of activities has been generously undertaken by dedicated and enthusiastic teachers. If it is to be placed on a sound footing as the necessity, not the luxury, of the educational service, then the restructuring of the professional ranks must be guaranteed.

What, next, could an authority do to prepare its teachers or prospective teachers for what, to many, would be an unaccustomed role? The 'deprofessionalised' teacher would be acutely sensitive and briskly adaptable to the culture in which he found himself teaching, both in terms of a varying curriculum (approach and substance) and a teaching relationship with adults as well as children. Most training schemes in this country reflect the earlier complaint about uniformity of opportunity. They tend to project a conception of teaching by which, according to age and aptitude, a child may be taught the same material by the same methods wherever he is to be found. The concept of the child being affected by his surroundings has made reasonable headway, but principally in terms of how those same materials and methods might be moderated. The idea of seeing the child in his surroundings as the determinant of materials and methods is slower in taking root. It requires a change in the view of the aims of education, a change in the view of how curriculum and methodology are decided, and a change in the view of how parents fit into the process.

An authority might be well-advised to make overtures to a nearby college of education, and it may well have one within its portals which, under the reorganisation of teacher-training, might be amenable to such a pleasing courtship. If the community school needs community school-teachers, then community school-teachers need to be trained in colleges which, as institutions, recognise that they should themselves relate fruitfully to schools in communities. It would be advantageous if a particular college of education could gear itself to producing the teachers for a particular authority. The general style, approaches and theories of that authority could be incorporated in the teacher-education programme, and, most useful of all, school practices for the student could be conducted in the authority's schools, offering them a foretaste of the peculiar delights in store.

The authority itself might be able to take advantage of the proposed pre-training higher education diplomas by offering them in the community colleges. Some recruitment might then commence on the basis of a higher education begun in the hurly-burly of rubbing shoulders with adolescent plumbers and artistic old age pensioners. This might avoid some of the preciousness of the exclusively teacher-student establishment.

The opposite fault could be an inbreeding, with Coketown producing teachers whom only Coketown knew. A flow of fresh immigrant teachers should be maintained, with both the appropriate college of education and the normal staffing procedures operating policies of external recruitment.

These would be straws in the wind, not rigid rulings, but an authority with a definite and clearcut policy must endeavour to influence training where possible, to avoid tremors at a later date for its young teachers and itself. It is, naturally enough, in the in-service field that the authority can really make felt its presence. Encouraged by all the relevant passages in the government White Paper, *Education: A Framework for Expansion*, and the James Report on teacher-training, it should adopt massive programmes of in-service training.

My own view is that the chief peril to progressive educational reform in this country is the failure to recycle staff when changes are made. One could muster several examples: the move from formal to informal primary approaches; the coming of ROSLA and secondary curriculum reform generally; the proclivity towards open-plan away from closed-wall schools; the introduction of modern maths or environmental studies or social education or realistic approaches in reading and language work; the challenge of mixed ability as opposed to streamed groups; the advent of intensified home-school relations, and the appointment of special officers, such as educational visitors; principally, the comprehensivisation of secondary education. In all these cases, thousands of teachers, reared for years under one dispensation, have been, overnight, expected to operate what sometimes is the direct opposite of all that habit, instinct and precept had instilled into them.

An enormous programme of recycling by in-service workshops, conferences, courses and seminars would be the initial and the continuing premier task of any authority wishing to commit itself wholeheartedly to community education. There is good will in the teaching profession and some recognition of the changes that are necessary, both among older teachers, mellow and astute in experience, and among that heartening wave of young teachers, with their high-toned social conscience. That is not to say that humans can, like some other forms of matter, be automatically recycled. Some teachers are notoriously tardy in their welcome of change, and, like other professionals, they seem to suffer an innate conservatism. What in-service training, on an adequately large-scale, may promise is that it will give tools and skills to those anxious to commit themselves fully to a community education campaign; it will give survival kits to those on the middle ground who are not too fussed either way; and it will give the diehards little leeway to complain that no one had ever helped them to grasp the new techniques.

A sizeable segment of this in-service training could be accomplished at community level, rather than authority level. Here, under the watchful guidance of the community education officer and his henchmen, the three organisers, it would be the concerted development of the school or college teams, rather than the development of the individual teacher, which would be paramount. More and more in-service work needs to be of this genre, with staffs and groups of staffs resolving the issues of their children in their community, together in solid professional co-operation.

This recycling policy alone points to a lengthy time-scale for the inauguration of this grand policy of educational regeneration. According to the conditions prevailing, one might estimate that most authorities in the United Kingdom embarking on a fullblooded exercise in institutional reform and its allied managerial changes would have to labour over a five- to ten-year period. There is nothing slight nor flibbertigibbet about community education. It is not a newfangled modification or fashion which one might add on or try out occasionally. It is, in short, a major, maybe a total, realignment of the organisation and the corpus of education. To attempt a sudden coup, prescribing fresh labels and merely creating a paper tiger, would be unworthy and possibly dangerous. A balance of boldness and care, coupled with a thoroughness of purpose and implementation, is, if slower, a safer and more stable approach.

Chapter 9

A General Policy of Community Development

A uniform pattern of community control is both impossible and undesirable. It is impossible for all kinds of historical, geographical, physical and human reasons, of a kind described in the early sections of this book. It is undesirable because these varying factors enable that spontaneous growth which is of the essence in any populist pattern of responsibility. It is the very natural bounds of human and group identity which are of most value, whereas the synthetic, over-rational and faceless segments for local governance sometimes carved out lack that kind of personal focus. Granted that important reservation, it might still be profitable to erect a general outline of community development, in part as a sounding-board for discussion and in part as a frame of reference for reform.

It was earlier suggested that the chief obstacles down the evolution-ary route from centralism to communalism were the clash between representative and participatory authority, consequent upon the need for large-scale services, and the latent contest between professional and layman. The previous two chapters have attempted to offer a practical solution, embracing some answer to both those problems. The major theme of this whole analysis, however, has been the inter-connectedness of all types of social provision. This applies both to the form in which the problem makes itself manifest and also to the style of the public or other response. It was suggested that this arose from the basic nature of civilisation, and its consistent attempt to equate its unavoidable, perhaps indispensable, inequality with a social policy that sustained that condition in as harmonious a manner as possible. It was further urged that, not only because principles of social justice were at stake, but because social expediency—the need to preserve that basic stability of our nation-state and its cash-economy—also pressed the point, the occasion was ripe for swing to community development.

Over against the see-saw of Whitehall-town hall, a policy of 'concentric circles' was mooted, with services democratically controlled for and by populations appropriate to the effective deployment of that service. Over against the possible friction betwen professional and layman, a policy of 'deprofessionalisation' was proposed, with the expert viewing his primary role as the acquaintance of the clientele with skills and understanding in his own field. The detail of these twin policies in terms of the education service was next described, but the schooling of children and of adults was never examined *in* social *vacuo*. The assumption was that, as educationists were about the task of community education, others would similarly be applying themselves to the job of community law and order, community health and so forth.

Social provision (or lack of it) is a circular business. Community education should enable people to make more effective choices and take more efficient action about an economy, a retail system, a transport service, a welfare programme and all the other socio-economic agencies which should be permitting them to participate more fully; as these more competent skills come into play, so, in turn, should the education institutions grow in wisdom and stature. More pessimistically, the downward spiral is equally telling. Lack of such skills inhibits folk from making valid selections and indulging in rational action in socio-economic spheres, where, in any case, little is being done to improve their participation, and, with each half-baked attempt so to become involved, the chances of their being allowed to is constantly diminished; in turn, the school suffers from lack of change and pressure in its social catchment and remains closed-in and reluctant to offer children 'community' information and know-how. It is a complicated trudge around the socio-economic treadmill, but, at least, it is nearer the truth than those simplistic models whereby either the school (cause) determined society (effect) or society (cause) determined the school (effect).

In brief, it would not even be half the battle to reform the education system along the lines projected here; nor, incidentally, would it be much better to reform all the other socio-economic features, and leave education untouched. If the concept of a four-cornered overall problem—ignorance, poverty, crime, ill-health—be preserved, then reforming education might, on strict geometrical grounds, be a quarter of the battle! What is required is a global approach, with, ideally, reforms advanced on all fronts. The community's education board would then be but one of a number of similar agencies assigned to develop particular administrative specialisms for its neighbourhood. An initial aim would be lateral contact among these, perhaps presupposing some form of community council, which maintained a joint sense of purpose for them all.

This is very important. The old municipal authorities tended, and the new district authorities tend, to pursue separate objectives and there is not often much apparent togetherness. Community development calls for immense *simpatía* among departments. It is not just a question of ensuring there are no entanglements, like having a day nursery slap bang on top of a nursery school, or the library and the clinic squabbling over territorial rights. It is much more positive and intrinsic than this negative avoidance of snarl-up. For instance, a purpose-built community school might anticipate its library being a physical component of the public library, its medical room a section of the local clinic, its nursery provision adjacent to the shopping precinct or even female-labour intensive factory, its dining accommodation providing the neighbourhood with its restaurant, its recreational and sports amenities forming an integral fraction of the community's parks and leisure facilities . . . and so forth. That is to state the case merely from the school viewpoint. There is no reason why the school should be central to the plan: one might as well have taken the parks or the bus terminus as the nub of the illustration.

If the school, or any other local governmental amenity, is to be so interwoven with its fellow services, to the visionary extreme where it is difficult to assess where one stops and the next starts, then one is asking for a degree of co-operation among municipal departments which has rarely in the past been observed. To be just, some of the inhibitions are nationally moulded by legislation affecting such local departments, an argument in itself for transferring the seat of control to the base where control takes effect.

This next raises the question about relations between one 'concentric circle' and the next. If the seat and/or base of control for sewage disposal or water supply is so much larger than, say, the seat/base arena for a primary school, how should the connection be made? Although the 'village' may be too small to cope with motorway provision or hospital management, the 'village' is still affected by the major route planned through its midst or the length of time required to transport serious casualties to hospital. It is precisely in these fields of regional management—and hospitals and motorways are just two compelling examples out of several—that popular pressure and consumer involvement is at its worst. Few ordinary citizens would know who purported to be watching over water supply, or regional health, or sewage, upon their civic behalf. Sadly, it might be argued, not many more could name the managers of their local school, but, at least, they would have some idea of where to start that particular voyage of discovery.

Certainly the consultative process must dig deep into the grass-roots, with the 'village' having a valid and authorised say in the sewage disposal stakes as well as the 'region'. Something of this has already been uncovered in the proposed management of education, with, at the extremes, the pre-school, the five-fourteen school, the post-school or college and possibly the polytechnic operating for gradually expanding layers of population. Throw in a regionally and nationally run pattern of higher and specialised education, and one might visualise the following administrative sequence:

Type of Area	Population	Function	Approx. Multiples
'Street/streets'	1,000	Pre-school	4 (45,000)
'Neighbourhood'	4,000	5–14 school	5 (11,250)
'Community'	20,000	Post-school/college	15 (2,250)
'Authority'	300,000	Polytechnic or equivalent	10 (150)
'Region'	13,000,000	Polytechnic, university or equivalent	15 (15)
'Nation'	50,000,000	University or equivalent	1 (1)

Many might flinch from the sheer quantity of units eventually involved, and recall the hundreds of agencies at parish and township level which bedevilled nineteenth-century and indeed twentieth-century local politics. But the beguiling and saving grace of a sequential system is that it is more rational and less random; it is honey-combed rather than haphazard. It could fit together in what, bearing in mind the very human and organic traits involved, could be a relatively symmetrical lock.

In everyday terms this asks for an administrative machinery which operates smoothly both in a lateral and a descendant direction. Just as there must, at any stratum of the administration, be intimate contact among services, so must there be as complete a relationship between strata. Now given what, on the face of it, would appear to be dozens of varied services from fire brigades to weights and measures and from cemeteries to street-lamps, this concept immediately looks unwieldly and overcomplex. If the six or so 'concentric circles' for education were merged and dovetailed, up or downwards and side-ways, with the 'concentric circles' of every other service, then a labyrinthine maze might emerge destined to ensnare even the most doughtily regulation-conscious local government officer. One might be warned by the notorious Oozlum Bird, which, many will recollect, flew in ever decreasing circles until overtaken by a bizarre and, biologically speaking, impossible mode of disappearance.

A possible consideration is that it is an unnecessarily large number of services which causes some of the trouble. Because there are many varying departments in local government, the problem of persuading them to work in co-ordinated fashion looks enormous, and the problem of inviting them also to operate through a series of tiers only adds to the enormity of the image. Certainly the prospect of a community of 20,000 contributing, fore and aft and left and right, to an intricate mesh of popular control over everything from dust-bins and crematoria to council house repairs and maternity wards is a trifle horrendous. Let us, however, postulate the alternative line of thought, whereby the number of services are reduced, or to be more accurate, encapsulated into a smaller number of unities. Truth to tell, certain authorities have already moved to a reduction of committees and a streamlining of departmental structures, in an effort to construct a logical and neat formula for local government organisation.

We began with the notion that, for formal analysis, social provision could be subdivided four ways, and that domestic government was concerned with its options on and response to the four major problems envisaged by that quadruple division. Could there, perhaps, be but four grand, all-embracing services, meeting the issues of poverty, ignorance, ill-health and crime? This would magically ease the entanglements of a myriad, whirling 'concentric circles'. At any one level there would be four, making it that much simpler for the four to interact across the managerial board and for each of the four to interact with the tier above and below. It would be a case of co-ordinating several of the existing services under one or other of the four headings. If each of these—education, health, law and order, and social welfare—is treated broadly and as an outgoing attack on the problem, and not just a narrow, even merely negative, response, then the four-part harmony takes on a more convincing form. One could argue about which goes where, but, as an early and deliberately inconclusive discussion-leader on the topic, the following breakdown of functions might serve. The lists would include presently run national and regional services, such as social security benefits, judicial procedures, the post office, hospitals and the like.

Education	*Public Order*	*Health*	*Social Welfare*
Education *per se*.	Police.	Planning.	Social services.
Libraries.	Fire.	Housing and building.	Welfare benefits.

Arts, entertainment, sports, parks, recreational and cultural services.	Weights and measures, food and drugs.	Water supply.
Communications (e.g. information services, post office, etc.).	Consumer protection.	Sewage and refuse disposal.
	Licensing and registration (e.g. births, electors etc.).	Health service and hospitals.
	Judicial agencies.	Cemeteries and crematoria.
	The legal management of government (e.g. town clerks and the like).	Clean air and other environmental services.

The missing element is plainly the economic one, and it is a vitally important one. In a thoroughgoing scheme of community development, one might expect to find some popular control of employment patterns and of retail trading and allied service industries. Public finance—the progenitor of all the other activities—is already part of the local government format, and this, too, must become engaged at varying consultative levels. If there is to be community industry and community trading, there should also be community transportation. Like finance, this is, of course, catered for in the public weal, with buses, trains, the licensing of taxis, the upkeep of highways and the construction of motorways. Obviously, transport overlaps the environmental field in that it is conducive or otherwise to good health. The fact that a motorway or a bus service has both a 'health' and an 'economic' character only underpins the urgent need to contract and conjoin service areas as neatly and simply as possible. For the moment, however, transport will remain in the economic sector.

If one takes a positive view of health and the necessity of viewing it in communal totality, then—and this was grudgingly accepted as long as a hundred years ago—housing becomes a public as well as a private domain, and the same applies to the other functions listed under 'health'. If one next applies that same argument to poverty and its treatment, then the analogy with a 'curative', as opposed to 'preventative' health service, is clear cut. As well as 'curing' poverty by handing out doles to social casualties or providing residential accommodation for those in desperate straits, one should be 'preventing' it by taking a grip of the economic fabric from which it emanates. By introducing whatever forms are feasible of popular consultation into employment and trading patterns, and developing those already existing in the public transport and civic finance fields, the problems of income and expenditure might be examined more radically, practically and positively at root. This argues the case for adding public finance, the retail and services trades, community employment and transport to the 'social welfare' list, on the straightforward grounds that poverty is about the work available, the wages paid, the prices and availability of goods, the cost and wherewithal of travel and the role played by governmental finance. This need not mean strict community control of the economy, either in its productive or servicing guises, but it does infer that the people should be free to enter into some dialogue about the placement and operation of jobs, shops and so on. Some—myself among them—would personally welcome moves to see the 'concentric circle' approach applied to the economy and the retail trade, so that workers' participation, community industry and transport and modern equivalents of the old style retail co-operatives might be introduced. But, as of this moment, that would stray outside the present ambit of governmental purview. It will have been noticed, of course, that an assumption has been made that nationally organised functions, such as the post office, would be susceptible to the new format, and, all in all, a continuum is suggested of ever-growing combines of area control over services critical and apposite for that areas's inhabitants.

How would this be organised for the mock-community of 20,000 souls, previously utilised to illustrate the educational aspects? This would be the actual 'community'; the central core of the proposed reform, holding the ground, as it were, between its components, the small neighbourhoods and localities, and the areas—authority, region, nation-state—which embrace it. There would be four agencies similar to the education board. The other three would be the health board, the public order board and the social welfare board. Like the education board, they would be comprised of elected members and professional officers. If the education board, in this ever more radical dispensation, now covered libraries, communication and leisure, adjustments would be required to the purely educational mechanism described in Chapter 8. Like the education board, the other boards would glean representation from the equivalent of contributory schools; like the education board, they would, in turn, seek representation at authority level. In the style of paper constitutions, one might hope that the four-part departmental structure would operate at authority level, and, in ever wider vision, at the regional and national tier, bearing in mind, of course, the basic point already stressed, in Chapter 8, about the nation-state, and then in descent, its lower strata institutions being providers and assessors and not deciders and enactors.

A corporate community of 20,000 inhabitants might thus seize and sustain democratic and participatory control of the following services at the designated level:

1. *Education Board*
   A community college and its feeder schools and pre-schools, as outlined in Chapter 8; plus a branch library, a cultural-recreational nexus; the community newspaper and/or other media and advice/information points; ideally, a sub-post office.

2. *Public Order Board*
   A sub-police station and, preferably, magistrate's court, with legal aid and advisory facilities attached; plus a section of the probation and allied services; a licensing and registration office or facility; a consumer unit (e.g. weights, measures, standards, trades descriptions, etc.), a sub-fire station, if appropriate. This board might also embrace the overall executive for the community council, that is the decentralised equivalent of the town clerk or chief executive.

3. *Health Board*
   A community clinic, preferably, group surgery; a comprehensive housing office; an amenities unit to cover the locality's interest in street cleaning, pollution and refuse disposal, and also to represent the local point of view apropos water and sewerage provision etc.

4. *Social Welfare Board*
   Welfare benefits and comprehensive social work and care facilities, plus the financial unit for the community; and whatever directive can be found and maintained over the siting and character of the retail trade, employment, economic enterprises and transport in the community.

Each board would have its chief officer, that is its community public order officer, a community health officer and a community welfare officer as well as a community education officer. A community co-ordinator—that is, a mini-town clerk—could co-ordinate their endeavours. At authority level there would be, analogous to the polytechnic, the hospital, the main police station, the central library, the general hospital, the bus depot, the general post office, and so forth. They would be managed by something similar to the authority's education committee, with delegates from the community tier representing their areas.

All that has been suggested about the role of the teacher would find echoes among the other professionals in the community. Housing officers, doctors and nurses, policemen, social workers, librarians and the remainder of the genre would need to relate to the community in the same fashion as the new-style teacher. Each would become the appropriate craftsman for the community, each attempting to secure that dainty balance between guiding and raising the communal level of awareness in his particular sphere and responding sympathetically and sensitively to the needs of the host community. Just as there is an educative community, which determines much of what happens educationally, so is there a public order community, a health community and a social welfare community, each of them dictating the quality of that aspect of the community's life-style. It is not the police station or the hospital which decides to what extent ours is a law-abiding or a healthy society: it is the totality of society's experience in regard of public order or public health which does this. It is the task of the specialist to deploy his expertise to monitor, steward and convene that 'community' and, needless to say, oversee its intermingling with the other 'community' layers.

Some of these schedules smack of contrivance and a hollow theoretical character. The very points made in part one about the natural unrolling of the organic, historical process may seem, to some, to be flaunted. That argument would, to some extent, be conceded. The concept of the four-part departmental structure and the detailed allocation of services was purely included as but one example of how such affairs could be arranged. It was included to demonstrate how the principles enumerated for education were viable for other governmental functions and how the necessary interaction of those functions could be managed. It may have had an air of artificiality, but it was intended as a sample response to an extremely natural and organic series of issues. Historically, there would now appear to be a social and political climate which calls for major forms of decentralised or community governance, albeit within the framework of a nation-state and a money economy. If that is true, then the managerial moulds required will not arise spontaneously, or if they do, they may well be haphazard and uneven . . . It is important, then, to debate and analyse whatever formulae may be needed to recast the old institutions.

To put it negatively, it is highly likely, that, if such attempts are thwarted or neglected, social injustice will continue and perhaps increase, and social dislocation will continue and perhaps increase. It is not uncommon, in the historical record, for social expediency and political philosophy to march hand-in-hand. In our present condition a form of community development may be our chief bulwark against social and political decline and instability, and, with its characteristics of popular democracy, grass-roots consultation and a reappraisal of egalitarian politics, it represents a very meaningful political mood of the moment.

In a sense, the form of community development is not so important as its attitude. Two elements have been earmarked as of chief emphasis: first, the 'concentric circle' counter to the oscillations of the central-local dichotomy; and second, the replacement of representative government by popular government. This totally alters the professional-client relationship. It at once places the professional in a blurred or, at best, overlapping, rather than in an acutely segregated, relation with everyone else. It calls upon the professional to link with others, above, below and to the sides, and, more significantly, it calls upon him to demythologise his expertise. Popular oversight must be based on informed, competent and skilled decisions, options and choices, and it would be a major aspect of the 'community' professional's task to guarantee that participatory democracy would thus be properly serviced. To revert to the educational example, one cannot have community schools and community education unless one has community school-teachers. Being a community school-teacher means having an attitude of mind and a particular belief about the way in which the educational process unfolds. What actual organisational pattern is decided upon is not unimportant: the structure would inhibit or encourage teachers according to its disadvantages or advantages. But the style and philosophic standpoint of the teacher—and of all the other professionals associated with social provision—is immensely critical. Indeed the community development movement may succeed or not according to the dispatch and thoroughness with which the cohorts of expertise can be re-cycled or re-educated to man the brand-new, profound and vastly different requirements of a public granted responsibility for its own decision-making.

Bibliography

Armytage, W. H. G., *Four Hundred Years of English Education* (CUP, 1965).

Atkinson, A. B., *Poverty in Britain and the Reform of Social Security* (CUP, 1969).

Ball, C. and M., *Education for a Change* (Penguin, 1973).

Birch, R. C., *The Shaping of the Welfare State* (Longman, 1974).

Blackstone, T., *A Fair Start: The Provision of Pre-School Education* (Penguin, 1971).

Boyd, W., *History of Western Education* (Blackett, 1947).

Brown, M., *Introduction to Social Administration in Britain* (Hutchinson, 1969).

Bruce, M., *The Coming of the Welfare State* (Batsford, 1961).

Centre for Educational Research and Innovation, *Equal Educational Opportunity* (OECD, 1971).

Clarke, J. J., *A History of the Local Government of the United Kingdom* (Jenkins, 1955).

Coates, R. and Silburn, S., *Poverty, the Forgotten Englishman* (Penguin, 1970).

Craft, M. *et al.*, *Linking Home and School* (Longman, 1967).

Craft, M., *Family, Class and Education,* (Longman, 1970).

Davie, R. *et al.*, *From Birth to Seven* (National Children's Bureau, Longman, 1972).

Dewey, J., *The School and Society* (CUP, 1900).

Dewey, J., *Democracy and Education* (Macmillan, New York, 1916).

Dicey, A. W., *Law and Public Opinion in England* (Macmillan, 1905).

Douglas, J. W. B., *The Home and the School* (MacGibbon & Kee, 1964).

Douglas, J. W. B., *All Our Future* (Davies, 1968).

Fantini, M. D. and Weinstein, G., *The Disadvantaged: Challenge to Education* (Harper & Row, 1968).

Finer, H., *The Theory and Practice of Modern Government* (Methuen, 1950).

Finer, S. E., *The Life and Times of Sir Edwin Chadwick* (Methuen, 1952).

Freire, P., *Pedagogy of the Oppressed* (Herder & Herder, (1970).

Garner, N. *et al.*, *Teaching in the Urban Community School* (Ward Lock Education, 1972).

Goodacre, E., *Home and School Relations: A List of References* (Home and School Council, 1968).

Goodhart, A. L., *English Contributions to the Philosophy of Law* (OUP, 1948).

Goodlad, S. (ed.), *Education and Social Action* (Allen & Unwin, 1975).

Gregg, P., *The Welfare State* (Harrap, 1967).

Gross R. and B. (ed.), *Radical School Reform* (Gollancz, 1971).

Halèvy, E., *The Growth of Philosophic Radicalism* (Faber, 1924).

Hall, P., *The Social Services of Modern England* (Routledge & Kegan Paul, 1970).

Halsey, A. H. *et al.*, *Social Class and Educational Opportunity* (Heinemann, 1956).

Halsey, A. H. *et al.*, *Education, Economy and Society* (Collier-Macmillan, 1961).

Halsey, A. H., *Educational Priority*, Vol. 1, *EPA Problems and Policies* (HMSO, 1972).

Hiemstra, R., *The Educative Community* (Professional Educators Publications, Nebraska, 1972).

Houghton, V. and Richardson, K. (ed.), *Recurrent Education* (Ward Lock Education, 1974).

Illich, I., *Deschooling Society* (Harper & Row, 1971).

James Report, *Teacher Education and Training* (HMSO, 1972).

Jencks, C., *Inequality: A Reassessment of the Effect of Family and School in America* (Basic Books, New York, 1972).

Jones, K. (ed.), *The Year Book of Social Policy in Britain 1972* (Routledge & Kegan Paul, 1973).

Kellmer Pringle, M. L., *Deprivation and Education* (Longman, 1965).

Kellmer Pringle, M. L. *et al.*, *11,000 Seven-Year-Olds* (Longman, 1966).

Kelsall, R. K. and H. M., *Social Disadvantage and Educational Opportunity* (Holt, Reinhart & Winston, 1971).

Kincaid, J. C., *Poverty and Equality in Britain* (Penguin, 1973).

Kuhn, T., *The Structure of Scientific Revolutions* (Chicago University Press, 1970).

Lakatos, I. and Musgrave F., *Criticism and the Growth of Knowledge* (CUP, 1970).

Laski, H. J., *A Grammar of Politics* (Allen & Unwin, 1925).

Laski, H. J. *et al.*, *A Century of Municipal Progress* (Allen & Unwin, 1938).

Lauwerys, J. A. and Scanlon, D. G. (ed.), *Education in Cities* (Evans Bros, 1970).

Lawrence, F., *The Origins and Growth of Modern Education* (Penguin, 1970).

Lawson, J. and Silver, H., *A Social History of Education in England* (Methuen, 1973).

Leigh, A. (ed.), *Better Social Services* (NCSS, 1973).

Lester Smith, W. O., *Government of Education* (Penguin, 1965).

Lovett, T., *Adult Education, Community Development and the Working Class* (Ward Lock Education, 1975).

MacDonagh, O., *A Pattern of Government Growth* (MacGibbon & Kee, 1961).

McGeeney, P., *Parents are Welcome* (Longman, 1969).

Martin E. W. (ed.), *Comparative Development in Social Welfare* (Allen & Unwin, 1972).

Marwick, A., *Britain in the Century of Total War* (Bodley Head, 1968).

Midwinter, E. C., *Priority Education* (Penguin, 1972).

Midwinter, E. C., *Projections: An Educational Priority Area at Work* (Ward Lock Education, 1972).

Midwinter, E. C., *Social Environment and the Urban School* (Ward Lock Education, 1972).

Midwinter, E. C., *Patterns of Community Education* (Ward Lock Education, 1973).

Midwinter, E. C. (ed.), *Pre-School Priorities* (Ward Lock Education, 1974).

Musgrave, P. W., *The School as an Organisation* (Macmillan, 1968).

Passow, A. H. (ed.), *Education in Depressed Areas* (Columbia University, 1963).

Plowden Report, *Children and Their Primary Schools* (HMSO, 1967).

Polyani, K., *Origins of Our Time: The Great Transformation* (Gollancz, 1945).

Poster, C., *The School and the Community* (Macmillan, 1971).

Rawls, J., *A Theory of Justice* (Harvard University Press, 1971).

Raybould, G. G., *Trends in English Adult Education* (Heinemann, 1959).

Raynor, J., *The Middle Class* (Longman, 1965).

Raynor, J. and Harden, J., *Cities, Communities and the Young* and *Equality and City Schools*, Vols 1 and 2 of *Readings in Urban Education* for the Open University (Routledge & Kegan Paul, 1973).

Rée, H., *Educator Extraordinary: The Life and Achievement of Henry Morris* (Longman, 1973).

Rennie, J. *et al.*, *Social Education: An Experiment in Four Secondary Schools* (Schools Council, Evans/Methuen, 1974).

Roberts, D., *Victorian Origins of the British Welfare State* (New Haven, 1960).

Robson, W. A. and Crichy, B., *Future of the Social Services* (Penguin, 1970).

Rooke, P., *The Growth of the Social Services in England* (Weidenfeld & Nicholson, 1968).

Rose, G., *The Working Class* (Longman, 1968).

Russell Report, *Adult Education: A Plan for Development* (HMSO, 1973).

Schools Council, *Enquiry: Young School Leavers* (HMSO, 1968).

Seebohm Report, *Local Authority and Allied Personal Services* (HMSO, 1968).

Sharrock, A., *Home and School:* An Annotated Bibliography (NFER, 1971).

Silver, H., *The Concept of Popular Education* (MacGibbon & Kee, 1965).

Slack, K., *Social Administration and the Citizen* (Michael Joseph, 1968).

Society of Education Officers, *Management in the Education Service*, (Coventry, 1974).

Tawney, R. H., *The Acquisitive Society* (Bell, 1921).

Tawney, R. H., *Equality* (Allen & Unwin, 1931).

Taylor, G. and Ayres, N., *Born and Bred Unequal* (Longman, 1969).

Taylor, W. (ed.), *Towards a Policy for Teacher Education* (Butterworth, 1969).

Titmuss, R. M., *Problems of Social Policy* (Longman, 1950).

Titmuss, R. M., *Essays on the Welfare State* (Allen & Unwin, 1958).

Titmuss, R. M., *The Irresponsible Society* (Fabian Society, 1959).

Titmuss, R. M., *Income Distribution and Social Change* (Allen & Unwin, 1962).

Titmuss, R. M., *Commitment to Welfare* (Allen & Unwin, 1968).

Tizzard, B., *Pre-School Education in Great Britain* (SSRC, 1974).

Townsend, P., *Poverty, Socialism and Labour in Power* (Fabian Society, 1967).

Townsend, P. and Bosanquet, N. (ed.), *Labour and Inequality* (Fabian Society, 1972).

Vaizey, J., *Education for Tomorrow* (Penguin, 1962).

Van der Eyken, W., *The Pre-School Years* (Penguin, 1967).

Ward, C. and Fyson, A., *Streetwork: The Exploding School* (Routledge & Kegan Paul, 1973).

Webb, G. and B., *English, Local Government* (Cass, 1929).

West, E. G., *Education and the State* (Institute of Economic Affairs, 1965).

Westwood, L. J., *Teachers: Their Role in School and Society* (Macmillan, 1969).

White Paper, *Education: A Framework for Expansion* (HMSO, 1972).

Williams, G., *The Coming of the Welfare State* (Allen & Unwin, 1967).

Wilmott, P., *The Evaluation of a Community* (Routledge & Kegan Paul, 1963).

Wiseman, S., *Education and Environment* (Manchester University Press, 1964).

Young, M., *The Rise of the Meritocracy* (Thames & Hudson, 1958).

Young, M., *Innovation and Research in Education* (Routledge & Kegan Paul, 1967).

Young, M. and McGeeney, P., *Learning Begins at Home* (Routledge & Kegan Paul, 1968).

Index